Be Still, Behold *and Dance* to the Divine

To my beloved brother Scott
who has blessed me
by his sincere, coura-
geous presence.
          I love you,
          Mark

BY THE AUTHOR

Nuggets of Spirit on the Run

Seven Spiritual Shortcuts to the Heart

MARK LeCLAIR DeGANGE

Be Still, Behold

and *Dance*

to the Divine

MAKING DAILY ACTS
A HEARTFELT SPIRITUAL
PRACTICE

LeClair Publications
Jacksonville

LeClair Publications
Jacksonville, FL 32207

Copyright © 2017 Mark LeClair DeGange

Cover design: ebooklaunch.com and Maria DeGange
Book interior: Andrea Reider
Editing: Kimberly Ashley Smith, Nancy Purcell, and Brad Kuhn, all of Jacksonville, Florida

Library of Congress Cataloging-in-Publication Data
DeGange, Mark LeClair, 1953-
    Be still, behold and dance to the divine : making daily acts a heartfelt spiritual practice /
    Mark LeClair DeGange.
        p. cm.

`ISBN 978-0-9993835-0-6 (paperback)
ISBN 978-0-9993835-1-3 (eBook)
1. Spiritual Life. I. Title
BISAC: BODY, MIND & SPIRIT / General. | BODY, MIND
& SPIRIT / Healing / Prayer & Spiritual. | BODY, MIND &
SPIRIT / Mindfulness & Meditation. | SELF-HELP / Meditations.
| SELF-HELP / Personal Growth / General. | SELF-HELP /
Spiritual.

Library of Congress Control Number: 2017914437

Printed in the United States of America

10 9 8 7 6 5 4 3 2

I am eternally grateful for my best friend and
loving wife, Maria; for Georgie, my gentle son;
and for Natalia, my wonderfully spirited daughter,
for teaching me in your special ways
the heart of the spiritual journey.

You are the dearest gifts of God I can imagine.

CONTENTS

Introduction xi

BE STILL

CHAPTER 1: DIVINE BASICS 1

One Morning in Communion with You 3
Glories of Thought 5
Lord and Love, One and All 9
Creation Is 11
Let There Be Light 15
Q&A: A Spiritual Life 21
A Divine Bill of Rights. 29
MEDITATION I Am the Light of Love 31

CHAPTER 2: WAKE UP 33

Shake Off the Dream 35
Below the Firmament 37
Waking Up Gently. 41
Order in My Bunk. 47
I Forgot? 53
Oh, to Be Out of My Mind 57

Mr. Lonely. 63
Why Kowtow to a Number 71
MEDITATION Conscious Care 76

CHAPTER 3: SOUL OFFERINGS. 79

Ascending Arc. 81
The Point 85
This Voice. 89
A Trail of Your Glory. 93
The Grove. 97
What My Life Would Look Like. 103
MEDITATION Soul Expression. 104

CHAPTER 4: AWESOME YOU. 107

Morning Listening Prelude 109
Permission to Be. 111
Welcome Gena 115
Incomparable You. 119
Have You Noticed 125
MEDITATION The Greatest Story Ever Told. . 127

BEHOLD

CHAPTER 5: THE HEART OF IT ALL. 131

Love One Another. 133
Hugs, not Heads. 137

Applying Gandhi to a Fault............ 141
The Art Is in the Heart 145
Starving at the Feast.................. 149
Self-Justified and Nowhere to Go......... 155
Handholding on High.................. 161
MEDITATION The Universal Glue 168

CHAPTER 6: REVELATIONS—
INSTANT AND OTHERWISE 171

The Hands of the Director 173
Toilet Training 179
A Revelation of Delays 183
On Being Ripe 187
The Price of Paint Removal............ 191
Turning the Shroud Around 197
From God 201
MEDITATION Listening for Wisdom....... 206

CHAPTER 7: GRACE................... 209

A Grace So Soon..................... 211
This Is How We Fit 215
A Wall or a Bridge................... 219
Coincidences, not Accidents........... 225
Death as a Way of Life 233
Oh, Wow! Leonids Is Back in Town........ 239
MEDITATION Grace and Ease 242

CHAPTER 8: THE JOURNEY HOME 245

The Royal Way 247
Crane Vistas 251
The Javelin, the Greenhouse, and the
    New Man. 259
Dishwashing Your Way to Nirvana or
    Taking the Grudge out of Zen 265
Loving Duty 269
Calling All Superheroes 275
Correction on I-95 South 281
You Are Home. 285
Her Arms Were Always Around Me 291
MEDITATION Always Home. 294

DANCE TO THE DIVINE

It Boils Down to Caring. 297

Further Thoughts. 302

INTRODUCTION

B e *Still, Behold and Dance to the Divine* came out of a spiritual journey begun in the early 1980s that continues to this day. It has been a process of mining and refining the meat of my experiences into spiritual insights and metaphors that can inspire and uplift others. These inspirations are fashioned in a way that will resonate with anyone who sincerely desires to go deeper to discover the beauty life holds. In one of the last stories, "You Are Home," for example, I discover that the quest for a life without limits alluded to in "Wake Up" has led me to the El Dorado of relationships, the love of family.

Throughout the book, two recognizable themes come to light: a Zen-like awareness of the activity at hand and the realizations that awareness give rise to. The task may be totally mundane, like picking up shattered glass, but staying present while picking it up can change you. The point is to wake up and milk the moment and not be bogged down nor dismissive of whatever is in your path. Each moment becomes an opportunity to give your heart and be transformed.

Part I

Be Still is the more metaphysical, poetic, and stage-setting section of the journey. The first chapter reads like an anthem to the Divine; next, come the wake-up calls that lift the sleep out of our eyes; following are soul offerings, which lead into the fourth chapter's rallying cry to the greatest story ever told, You. Because Part 1 focuses on the more thought-provoking divine basics, I encourage you to give yourself time to reflect on the ideas of this section before jumping into the next.

Part II

Behold gets you right onto the spiritual playing field and into the substance of the path—relationships. This universal subject we all deal with touches various life experiences, some quite familiar to you and others perhaps not; yet they traverse the same concern, Am I building bridges to myself, my neighbor, and God by my attitudes? The self-awareness that unfolds comes on the shoulders of work or are strokes of Grace. Either way, they are the heart's way of declaring that you are home.

The Divine Deepening following each entry brings together the idea of the sayings on the page across from the poems or stories and the texts themselves and are meant to open a spiritual dialogue within you.

Hopefully, they will make what has been written more real for you. The Meditation at the end of each chapter deepens your reflection on the insights you've just delved into.

Part III

Dance to the Divine is my way of answering the question, "What keeps us in the game?" It's easy to be "all in" when fulfillment and spiritual satisfaction are evident. But why commit our hearts to situations and relationships that seem unrewarding, demeaning, and stretch our patience to the moon for no good reason? Why *Be Still*? What is to *Behold*? What is to gain?

Enjoy the journey in the following pages. I am excited to imagine how something you read will elicit one, two, three, even a bucket load of personal revelations. What if that insignificant event secretly lit your fire and you just hadn't acknowledged it at the time? What if it could change your life simply by putting some attention on it? Maybe it's time to dust it off. Write it down. Maybe it's time to be unselfish and place the light on the riches you know so well. Maybe you are the spark that will call others to the Light.

BE STILL

1

CHAPTER

DIVINE
BASICS

First the Thought
then the Word
then the "Wow."
Thanks be to God.

ONE MORNING IN COMMUNION
WITH YOU

You, Love, aim of my loftiest phrase
Whose heights ever soar above right praise
Bless my soul's journey that I lay bare
So others may know proofs of your care.

DIVINE DEEPENING
Try your hand at composing a poem or prayer
to the Divine, whatever the term *Divine* means
to you. (*Love* is the first term for the Divine
that comes to me.)

*Look how much nature gives
and how little it demands.
A tree offers without attitude.*

GLORIES OF THOUGHT

Morning mounts the dawning rays of the sun
Seeding the horizon in glories of thought

A songbird catches the glory
Candidly sitting a sec
On a shrub top trilling and spilling
Throat-clearing, piccolo-perfect melodies:

"Wake up, wake up,
Wake all ye up
Now is day, in display
Come and play, to the day
Wake up, wake up,
Wake all ye up"
              off he goes.

The meadow rolls out her finery
In perfect sync with the morn's
Facade of fast fading mist

Flower tufts pop out in
The simplest of painted debuts
Who can match their offering?

The *ahh* lush meadow grass
Is dressed up to an edge
In lustrous beaded overcoats of dew

A stand of sturdy oaks and maples
Announces its perennial guard
At the meadow's western edge

And I'm on a rock, gazing
Like a king who takes in
His waking kingdom

           Then
A freshly inspired breeze
Tickles by my nose
Like a pied piper with a
Floral scent in tow
               and quickly vanishes
Into a reminder of its ethereal beauty

All glory be to God.

DIVINE DEEPENING

Go out into nature. Suspend opinions.
Befriend a tree, bush, flower, or stream.
What life-giving, spiritual qualities does it
embody that ennoble your own heart?

*Can we all agree (for once) that
the least common denominator
of every thought, word, and deed
in the sacred and profane is Love
and go from there?*

LORD AND LOVE, ONE AND ALL

You are my flame, O Presence
You are my fire
You are the Love that holds
    my heart on high
You are my sight, O Radiance
You are my sun
You are the Light of good
    that never fades
You are my life, O Munificence
You are my legions
You are the Grace of days
    and nights supernal
You are my soul, O Resplendence
You are my seasons
You are the glowing sense
    of joy eternal

You are my speech, O Eloquence
You are my silence
You are the mighty voice
    whispering tenderly
I am Lord and Love, One and All.

DIVINE DEEPENING
What is the prime motivator
in your life? Be honest.
Is it working well for you?

I am inspired by Spirit, being
Its exhalation into the world.

CREATION IS ...

Creation is my word play, grasping at what probably can never be fully grasped.

Creation is Mozart transcribing the celestial rhapsodies of the universe and those notes being launched back into the universe when an orchestra begins to play.

Creation is Being's utterance, *I love,* as the totality of expression, the whole of consciousness.

Creation is the continuous revelation or unfolding of what Mind-Spirit-Life is.

Creation is the conscious expression of the light of good, radiantly reflecting God's glory.

Creation is the spirit (holy act) of Mind voicing its desire that there be . . . (*You fill in the blank and have a great time doing it!*).

Creation is the Force (divine Will) of Wisdom (divine Intelligence) emanating love.

Creation is
> Spirit animating Itself
> Mind knowing Itself
> Love loving Itself
> Soul being Itself.

Creation is I AM: The I—Creator, one God, the pluralistic Elohim—and the AM—creation, or man and the universe—forever expressing oneness.

Creation is the rejoicing of the lights of Light.

Creation is the fire of divine Intelligence speaking the Word of life.

Creation is a baby's cry eliciting a mother's tender embrace.

Creation is a yes, a no, a maybe so, and let's go.

DIVINE DEEPENING
Meditate on one (or more) of the
definitions of creation.
How does it apply to your creative process?

Imagine a ceaselessly renewed stream of loving light pulsating from the Source—that's you.

LET THERE BE LIGHT

L*et there be light.* Whatever we understand about these words, they are positive, direct, and loaded with *Yes* potential. If we choose to accept that these words are the Creator's eternally satisfied, primal command then we're off to a good start. They proclaim the universe as a creation of light, without a tinge of darkness. Light is the only essence that is. God commanded it and it's a done deal.

The world lives happily ever after in the light of being.

Not quite. Somehow, somewhere, in the creation story/myth/drama, man bought into the notion that walking in the light was out of vogue and that darkness was appealing as a way of being. You know the rest: Man's predilection for selfish, earthly power trips pervaded world history. He coveted land, and more land. He conquered by horrific slaughter; built empires propped up by slaves; served gods of gold and wealth; relegated women to baby-making menials; and justified his actions by religious and racial beliefs, which promoted separation rather than unity.

Yet how did darkness come in?

What happened to us? Did God rescind Its affirmation that creation was good? Why would we be fashioned from the one Light, and then somehow reconstituted as part light and part darkness? Did a supposed benevolent Creator lose control of creation? Banish Its very own? That would be Self-annihilation, like cutting off one of your own limbs. Perhaps it was our free will gone awry? Doesn't sound very free. Whatever the explanation is, man, like a misguided amnesiac, accepted the downgrade and fell for the shadows he mistook for his own soul.

The world and all its isms have strived their best to figure out the long, dark night of human history. Wars over resources, senseless violence, and racial and religious intolerances still being inflicted across the globe make anyone wonder if we'll ever escape this legacy of evil and find the way back to purity, innocence, goodwill. We won't, if we keep messing with *inherent evil* conceptions; we will, if we stand up for the declamation of what Source has made: man as a being that can only reflect the Light. Why fall for the world's ignorant, ill-directed struggle against sunken forms of self, or feel embarrassed about and shrink from the light that is inherently ours to stand in.

Aren't we here to embody the light? Recall what the Christ said, *I am the light of the world.* He remembered his spiritual nature, and never forgot. He wasn't fooled by the bevy of materialistic beliefs that came at him from the world around and by those closest. Instead he kept pointing out our true nature with such reminders like, *You are the light of the world . . . let your light shine before others . . . .* He included us in his glorious inheritance, and wouldn't settle for anything less in us.

While living in Boston many years ago I worked with AIDS sufferers at the Boston Living Center, a residential/outreach treatment program. Most participants accepted the fact that their immune systems were compromised and took an assortment of drugs (termed "cocktails") to combat their illness. I could have looked on them with the same set of beliefs and eyes, namely, they are sick, their immune systems are depressed, etc. It would have been normal. Instead, I took a different stance. It made much better sense to hold them in the light of perfection. I understood this would do a whole lot more to promote their well-being than if I added to the reality of the painful, earth-born story presenting itself. In fact the healthiest AIDS patient I worked with was a man who came in infrequently and was weaning himself off the cocktail regimen by living his life to the fullest. In other words, he was not settling for an exclusively AIDS identity, he was letting his light shine in the world.

Doesn't it feel more liberating to know that our endowment is from above—from the Source of light, which does not vary in the enduring quality of pure, unfettered light entrusted to each of us. Let's make it our primary job to see our seven-billion-plus brothers and sisters as translucent expressions of the one Light.

DIVINE DEEPENING

Name three conscious ways you cultivate
the light within.
How about three with the light in others?

You are the answer
your heart has been waiting for.

Q&A: A SPIRITUAL LIFE

Q. Does life have a purpose?
A. Love. Being love and sharing love—what could be more meaningful than that. Many lesser purposes come and go that turn us on and inspire, but in the end if love hasn't been at the center of our lives what's the hype been about. I like the title of a Bobby McFerrin hit song from years ago, *Don't Worry, Be Happy.* It puts obsessing about life in perspective. Don't worry about your purpose so much. Just be yourself and live. The joy of being you will lead to your highest contribution and bless the world.

Q. Do you recommend a particular spiritual practice?
A. Love God first. This keeps us on the right road in the midst of world attractions, commitments, etc. After that, one's practice is an individual thing. There are as many practices as there are people in the world. Each of us is a royal road in and to eternity. Our work is to wake up and realize that within ourselves we have everything needed to achieve harmony and bliss. The biggest prerequisites I see for a healthy spiritual life are honesty, humility, and love. It's what you bring to your practice that counts. Perseverance is essential too. Everyone on earth gets tested. Being steadfast in our practice buoys us in those tough times.

Meditation has been the heart of my practice for years, whether I am meditating on the Light within, on silence, on the nature of the Divine, on a sacred text, or on the task at hand. Meditation pervades my life.

Q. What is the ideal environment to do spiritual work?
A. For most, seclusion of some sort is necessary to spiritually connect. Establishing a quiet space in a corner of your house is a good way to ensure you have a place to go. Nature is ideal, too. The woods, a serene lake, or an undisturbed place in your backyard may help you feel the inner peace you seek. Being in the presence of a teacher who embodies qualities you aspire to greatly helps, as do communal prayer and worship, or meditation in like-minded groups. The important thing, though, is to sit down wherever you live—really, wherever you are—and ask deeply in your heart to be shown the way. Spirit is there filling the silence and waiting for you. Don't wait for ideal conditions. Jump in.

Q. What's your take on the spiritual and the material?
A. I hope I have not dichotomized the two in my life too much. Life has a spiritual basis to me. My thoughts, my breath, my actions are opportunities to express the one Spirit. Some people may look on life more from a material standpoint. That's understandable given the world's focus on position, money, fame, and lately perfectly chiseled bodies. But, a spiritual stance offers a way out of the stress of material striving. If worldly

success is yours, great. Embrace it. Shouldn't Spirit provide all we need and more? Yet, as we grow, the feeding of the inner life becomes the essential part of anything we are doing. The spiritual alchemist in us is ever on the job transforming experience into heartfelt reasons to cherish others.

Q. Is there a more suitable diet for a spiritual life?
A. This is a subject with many books full of opinions and theories to chew on. My approach is basic: Eat foods close to their natural state; drink enough water; be moderate; and especially hold peaceful and grateful thoughts when you eat.

Is being a vegetarian more conducive to spirituality than being a meat eater? I'd rather know what's in someone's heart than belly. Mindlessly sticking to a natural foods diet seems little better than putting away a hunk of meat and remembering to thank the animal for the sacrifice it made for you.

The foods we eat are not what spirituality is about. They're a good start in self-love. But it seems wiser to eat what's in front of us with appreciation than obsessing over whether the food is pure, adulterated, grown and picked by a loving farm worker or transported by a trucker who cusses his way across America (no offense to truckers; they blessed my hitchhiking days across America). We taint the food or allow it to nourish us more by what we bring to it. Didn't the Master Teacher say it's not what goes into your mouth that defiles you but what comes out of you?

I tend to forget about food when I am focused on projects. Though I enjoy eating the evening meal with my family. The togetherness is special, whatever we eat, and whether we talk much or not.

My dad didn't formally meditate; I couldn't tell if he prayed; and he wasn't much of a churchgoer at heart. But, was he ever in his element in the kitchen! When he cooked, the mouths of the angels were surely hanging open and drooling over his table. Pizza, breads, garden salads, raviolis, meatballs, and cheesecake were saturated with the juice of his creativity. It was like biting into consciousness. I am sure there was as much or more spirit and life in his preparation of cooked foods than in meals made by the most well-intentioned cook using organic this and organic that. It's simple: He loved to cook. And he loved to cook for others. Love was the chief ingredient, and we all tasted it.

Q. What do you look for in a spiritual teacher?
A. Love and lightness. Expressing love, wisdom, compassion, kindness, and so on are natural outcomes of our spiritual growth. The self has been abnegated to such a degree that the light of Spirit flows freely through it the way the sun flows freely through a clear windowpane. Be aware though that a spiritual teacher, just like you and me, is on the road and hasn't necessarily arrived at a final Truth. To me, every one of us teaches about Spirit simply by our presence. No

one has a greater market share of Spirit. Each of us is learning to allow Spirit to lead.

The teacher is waiting within.

Q. Where do relationships fit in?

A. This is the heart and soul of our existence as far as I'm concerned and we need to get it right. Otherwise, we play out our enlightenment selfishly yet don't know how to be close with others. I personally have had to reckon with this.

Then where do we begin?

At the top: God, Spirit, Source, Allah—the Divine. Anywhere else we turn we find shifting sands or shadows that don't hold up in the light. I'm referring to turning to the world as source, supply, and reason for being. It always changes. Name, fame, and wealth are not constants; they have their day and then slip into the shade. Spirit, our true life, is the constant. When we turn to the one omnipresent Spirit, we find love, wisdom, and strength.

Most spiritual paths now recognize God as infinite Love. They embrace the concept of supremely benevolent Being. Many of us, I know, were turned off by limited, false notions of deity. I'm speaking of the angry, distant, and patriarchal concepts of a god who becomes available when you die—if you've been halfway good. That sense is done. In its place is Father-Mother, supreme Intelligence, constantly watchful, all loving, and ready to supply our needs.

That's the most important relationship, getting our concept of God straightened out. Then comes us. How do we perceive ourselves? Can I truly love myself if I think that I am evil and naturally inclined to self-ishness and negativity? Doesn't that bring God—sup-posedly the only Creator—down with me? He allowed that! There goes a perfect God and His innocent child, man, out the window.

It makes infinitely more sense to establish man's rightful place as a child of the Almighty. How could the kingdom be within me unless I am fit for it? Impurity cannot inherit purity. Nor vice versa. We express good, we express forgiveness, we express kindness because they are the true principles of our being. Selfishness, hatred, and egoism belong to a self that is separate from harmony. These deluded states punish and ban-ish themselves from bliss by their very nature. It is our job to claim and maintain our loving nature.

The third aspect of the relationship triangle is oth-ers. This is the proof. You master this aspect of life and you've pretty much done it. Really, how can you fail? If you recognize your innocence and purity, how can you not see it in others? After all, you came from the same Source. That makes you brothers and sisters. Can you be fooled by another's clothes, schooling, speech, or position in life? They are earthly facades. What do they have to do with the heart? Nothing. So, don't be fooled. They pale next to a genuine smile. When someone gives you a big, loving smile, does anything else matter? Where does the divisiveness go? Where do character flaws go? Where does the supposed difference between you and them go? They dissolve. They were like shadows trying to stand in the sun. They can't. What's left are warm hearts beaming from soft eyes.

So, who are you willing to leave out in the cold, to forsake because they don't meet your critical standards? Can you afford to lose a single one of your fellow men? They are your ticket to enlightenment and they are standing right next to you.

DIVINE DEEPENING
What does a spiritual life mean to you?
Write down ways you are living it daily
and ways it affects your relationships.

When Love alights
fear falls unsound
folds into naught
thus never was
the way Truth taught.

A DIVINE BILL OF RIGHTS

I came from God. I live in God. I am inseparable from
God. Therefore, I am one with God.

I have a clear sense of God's reality; for S(He) gives it
to me.
All-loving, all-acting, all-powerful, ever-present God
is the only Life, the One I adore.

As God's expression, I reflect what God is—
Truth, Life, and Love.

I know God's perfect thoughts, hear God's truthful
voice,
see God's peaceful presence, and feel God's joyful
spirit.

My life is eternal; therefore, the substance of my
being is incorruptible, lasting, and real.

The world and its illusory changes cannot touch nor
harm me.

I live the law of divine Love, and love all beings as
my very own.

Love meets all my needs.
Love is Source, God, Universe, liberation.

I LOVE ♥

DIVINE DEEPENING
Let your soul speak and define your
divine bill of rights.
Write it down. Meditate on it daily for a week.
Edit as often as needed. Live it.

MEDITATION

I am the light of Love

Sit comfortably in a chair. Spine straight. Feet flat on floor. Take three slow 'n' easy belly breaths through the nose. Feel your body relax into the chair with each breath. Close your eyes.

Bring your consciousness into the center of the chest where the metaphysical heart is. Take a breath into it. Imagine a pure white glowing light there. Love the light. Feel grateful for it. Stay there a few minutes acknowledging the light as eternally yours.

When ready, quietly say *I am the light of Love*. Know that the Love you speak of is your divine spark, divinity Itself, always connecting you to life. Feel how calming that phrase is. Feel it softly vibrate in your chest. Say it again, and feel it resonate deeper into your chest and your being. Say it a third time, almost inaudibly, and **know that's what you are**.

See the light of Love fill your entire body right to the extremities. Experience all parts of you release as they are washed through by the light wave of Love. Be aware if any part of you, be it physical, emotional, or mental, is not being bathed in this light. Let the light suffuse there.

Let the phrase get softer and less frequent until it is an inaudible vibrating refrain. Watch the light of Love move outside your body and fill your aura in all six directions about three feet around you. See the light of Love brighten and strengthen your aura.

Now see it emanate from the center of your chest area like ripples emerging from the center of creation. Each time you think *I am the light of Love* watch those ripples move outward in concentric circles like waves through your home and to your loved ones, friends, and whoever else needs to receive the light of Love. Take your time. See where the light of Love wants to take you.

Come back to your body. Know that the light of Love you have activated both protects you and attracts those resonating on that high level. Feel grateful for the light of Love within. Ground the light of Love down through your legs into the earth. When ready open your eyes. The light of Love is all around you ready to serve you.

2

CHAPTER

WAKE UP

Security's illusion is tethered
to a person, place, or thing.
Security's reality is boundless
in Spirit.

SHAKE OFF THE DREAM

The struggle for what seems certain
Can saddle sense in grave mistakes
Or brings truth, which parts the curtain
To the life only Spirit makes.

So if we meet a worldly voice
Whose song is like a pleasing ode
Do we dance? Waver in our choice?
No. Spirit is our sure abode.

Arise! Shake off the dream darkly
Clothe yourself brightly in the Word
Sound the trumpets, scale the holy
Heights—this is the day of the Lord.

DIVINE DEEPENING
Define for yourself the difference between
what shackles you and what frees your spirit.

Do you grow straight up
like a redwood to the sun
in choosing your heart and not
list like a weed in the wind
to the fads of the day?

BELOW THE FIRMAMENT

The way of life is above to the wise, that he may depart from hell beneath

Proverbs 15:24

Below the firmament I saw a dense and deceptive, ground-clinging mist that held the groping and grappling masses to covet what they knew, the earth. The yelling and pushing of mad ambition into itself was like a snarling, frenzied marketplace one instant that wasted itself into an infatuated and fatiguing, dreamy foray in front of store windows to look and flirt with itself until that illusion wore off and it was time to leap into another and another, never satisfied, always searching for the next, the hottest, the latest and greatest.

These pathetic, prideful players continue striving to match the world's wishes. When they do, the world throws another angle, another fantasy, to indulge in. They in turn jump like ravenous carnivores ready to consume, but are consumed and don't know it.

Where is Love in this story? Has She abdicated to the wiles of Mara?* Has She given up on this world? No. She is right there, loving and watching patiently above the thick, chaotic din. Waiting for tired, dissatisfied humanity to wake up and do one simple, yet ground-shattering thing: poke their heads above the fear-fraught fracas and behold the light of day—Her smiling face. All it takes is a restless thought sparking a question then rejection of an enslaving habit. All it takes is a sincere cry for that which is good and lasting.

The divine Mother knows Her own, hears their cries. In Her grace is their life.

*In Buddhist cosmology the personification (demon) of greed, lust, delusion and death that tries to temp one off the path of enlightenment. The Buddha is said to have defied the assaults of Mara and his beautiful daughters to seduce and destroy him.

DIVINE DEEPENING

Is your discernment being clouded by
your appetite to consume?
If so, what do you need to do to regain self-mastery?

The gentle masters the jagged. *
(inspired by the Tao)

*Lao Tzu, *Tao Te Ching* (Nashville: Sam Torode Book Arts, 2009), 43.

WAKING UP GENTLY

What an incredible Christmas gift I got from my new cat, Zoe.

We put her out of our bedroom last night after I discovered her on her hind feet, reaching her paws into the aquarium. No way, you are not getting our fish, I thought, as I shooed her away.

We quickly fell back to sleep.

Shortly thereafter we sharply woke to a loud crashing of glass . . . Zoe! I flew out of bed, slid the bedroom barn door open and went downstairs to see the damage. None. I couldn't find any broken glass. That made no sense. As I walked up the stairs I glanced over at our open bedroom window and saw glass shards covering the balcony. Zoe had knocked one of the 8x8 glass blocks down on the balcony.

Glass blocks don't break, they explode and fracture into a million different-sized shards and flakes that can end up farther than you would ever imagine, including in the corners of a large living room and kitchen door below.

Fortunately, Zoe was unhurt.

When it was dawn, I gathered a work light, gloves, and garbage bag and went to work picking up glass from the balcony carpet. A few minutes into it I realized that my work gloves were too thick to easily pick up small pieces. Finer gloves were needed. But, I preferred bare hands.

YOU NEED TO BE GENTLE came to me as I was on my hands and knees. Maria, my wife, had said this to me the night before when I had apparently reached out impatiently and tilted upward my son's soup bowl so his free hand could feel the higher tilt necessary to easily scoop the last of his soup out. My ego had reacted, partly because her comments seemed unjustified when I was being caring enough to help and secondly, Was I so rough? I thought *that* Mark was dead. Maybe not.

I had a huge opportunity to practice as I had never practiced before. Shards of every conceivable angle of jaggedness presented themselves to me. I couldn't boldly thrust my hands through space and grab one, two or more pieces at a time. Notice the words, *boldy, thrust, grab*. If this is the way I wanted to do it, fine, I could, but I would learn nothing and feel the pain. I easily could put the work gloves back on, get the dust pan and brush, the vacuum cleaner, and be done with it. Weren't there better things to be doing with my life on a Friday morning. No. This was the door opening to self-mastery. I had to go through it. I knew the "gentle" prize in my development that waited.

Though I couldn't plan exactly how I would approach each shard, I could approach slower, I could pick up each piece more softly. I had to. I was pierced twice, once in the beginning when I was learning what this was all about, and the other time when I was near the end, thinking I knew it all and just wanted to be finished. In a few other instances, a tiny glass shard was stuck point first into my index finger. Strangely, I did not bleed.

I had to be present, and patient. There was no hurrying in and no hurrying out with the glass shards. Often, I needed to shift my head from angle to angle to see if the light caught any sharp glints from the carpet where I was working. Then I would go in with a steady, deliberate descent and use my thumb and index fingers like sensitive pincers and embrace the piece. The continual conscious act yielded some beautiful revelations.

- Each glass shard, in fact the whole process of the glass block smashing into thousands of large, small, and tiny sharp shavings and slivers, was a mirror of life's rougher, reactionary, and opinionated ways. I could bring my own edginess to it, and get into the blame game, or I could get on my hands and knees and bring my patience, presence, and surrender to the task.

- My soft, roundish fingertips were such a contrast to the jaggedness of the glass pieces. If I gently used my fingers and honored their softness, each time I picked up a shard of glass I felt its shape, but no pain. I neutralized the whole sharp experience.

- What if every piece was like the crying of a baby that has been splintered away from its mom? How would I treat it? Would I manhandle it and throw it into the garbage bag? No, I must pick it up with care, meekness, and respect. There mustn't be indifference and haste for the least of pieces. And when I put each of them into the bag I don't throw them, I place them. Otherwise, if I miss, it is again in the carpet somewhere and could call out for my attention in a painful way.

- Lastly, if what I was handling was gold, how would I touch it? Someone might say, I would scoop it up right-quickly. True. In this case, the gold idea focused my mind on the preciousness of the substance laying before me. I needed to savor it, as if each piece was invaluable. This negated the callousness of just picking up the next insignificant glass shard and instead inculcated the importance of every one of my actions and the part each piece played in it.

In the end I was very grateful for what the cat had done. Especially was I grateful for my growing consciousness of gentleness. It also taught me that I could approach the most unwanted task with harmony. In turn, it would both protect me and allow me to do the job thoroughly. Perhaps other men would be blessed by my practice of gentle, too.

DIVINE DEEPENING

Pick something you must do on a regular basis,
something you'd rather hurry through,
and commit your heart to it,
as if it is the most precious act you will ever do.
See what happens.

If Love governs all,
why don't I trust It
to run the entire show.

ORDER IN MY BUNK

As a child, I daily made the lower portion of the bunk where I slept as neatly as possible, carefully smoothing the creases. I didn't like creases. My brother, who slept on the top bunk, had a different ethic: He left things where he pleased. That was okay sort of, if it wasn't imposed on me. When he'd plop all over my bed and mess it up, I'd go nuts. It ruined the perfect smoothness. War was on.

A sense of order followed me into adulthood and still compels me to organize my environment, at least not leave my mess for someone else to take care of. Is it normal to demand order in my life? Should I worry that I have a problem? Believe that I'm *anal compulsive* or whatever correct label psychologists affix to someone who enjoys knowing where things are? I'm not burdened by order; should anyone else be? Can a love of order be turned into a *dis*order?

Since it is perfectly natural to neatly arrange my desk, tidy up the house entrance, and hang my clothes where I can find them, I'll proceed . . . and clean the cat litter box, organize my desk files, and so on. It never ends. Bringing order into our lives is a constant. You can vary the doing of it. But you can't avoid. You can resist it or take an opposite stance and refuse to throw the newspapers out. Guess what? Practice this long enough and you'll be competing with pounds and mounds of dailies and magazines for living space. Psychologists have a name for that, too.

For me, order is pleasing. Even lifting. When I walk into my home, I don't want my senses (mind) cluttered by chaos. A right sense of order is based on principles you see everywhere. Think about a healthy tree: It grows upward not downward. This maximizes its leaves' ability to absorb available sunlight. When the season cools, the tree pulls its life force in, drops the very leaves that helped feed it, and protects the once tender tips of its branches where leaves were.

A blind person, for instance, must put a premium on order too, or else lose things left and right and find nothing. If their bureau drawer is crammed helter-skelter with underwear, T-shirts, dress shirts, etc., it's touch madness. If the cheese is put away in the cupboard and not in the fridge, it will go bad, and there goes their favorite ham and cheese sandwich. Every aspect of their life is governed by this need for order. More importantly, if their room, kitchen, and bathroom are all perfectly in place, they still need an ordered thought process to function in that space.

An orderly universe speaks to me of an orderly Intelligence. A Supreme Governor who keeps the sun at the right distance from the earth, who keeps the oceans from overflowing the lands, and who imparts a higher law that guides the hearts and minds of billions of people who live crowded together in cities over the globe. Over seven million New Yorkers, for example, share the same small island, and literally live on top of each other. But they peacefully coexist for the most past. They must be guided by a Higher Intelligence.

I lived nearly a decade in New York and it was a rarity to witness violence. Subways were super crowded, and I rarely heard complaints. Streetlights went on every evening. Gas always flowed to my stove. Grocery stores never ran out of food. The streets were pretty clean. Clearly a working order was behind the scenes making services run harmoniously. If not, the City would have been a malfunctioning, anarchic mess, where walking across a street would have been like a sprint for survival.

To my sense of things, Love is the real animator of life. Love wisely orders our actions. Love creates businesses that serve our needs. Love impels us to be mindful of and caring for the neighbor next door. Love is the sacred order of life tending a babe in the womb.

Love makes our bed even when we don't want to.

DIVINE DEEPENING

Where can a love of order straighten out your life?

*Cross a rainy day
with someone's attitude
you get the attitude.
Then cross a sunny day
with the same attitude
you get the attitude.
Get it?*

I FORGOT?

"I forgot to thaw the chicken; now we'll have to throw something together fast otherwise we'll end up eating at eight o'clock."

"I forgot to tie my shoelaces and tripped and hurt my wrist."

"I forgot I had an appointment with a new client, and now I will be late."

Each of us could add our own infamous blunders of omission to the list, and it would probably stretch from New York to Alaska and back. We forget to prepare ourselves; we forget to be present enough to remember to do what was ours to do—and life slips on by.

Forgetfulness can get you going the wrong way. I remember having a sudden urge to get out of the City and see my folks in Connecticut. I got there, chilled, and was lounging around the next morning and suddenly leaped out of the chair and yelled, "I was supposed to work at *Sports Illustrated* today." I quaked, called, and fortunately received mercy from my boss.

Forgetting runs rampant like the plague, attaching itself subtly to our insides and gobbling up our consciousness before we even know there is something to remember. We might as well be sleepwalking. Life is merciful, though, and just as Life allows us to forget past traumas and foolishness, Life gives us another day and another opportunity to redo. The All-Wise is most patient with our self-centered gyrations through life.

It's our choice to either keep the forgetting ball numbly rolling along or to pause, be still and say *thank you* for the least little thing that Life reminds us to do. Better yet is to remember to be grateful for the challenging situations that rub against our likes and our game plan. This is tough remembering, the kind that I imagine brings us closer to our hearts as well as mastering the whims of desire.

My choice is to remember. Learning is lots easier than resisting, resenting, and repeating. Simply put, being fully here responding to what is mine is the right way to put the house in order. I don't want to burden my family or any others with the fallout of my forgetfulness; I'd rather leave a shine on the table. This is respect for who comes next. This is caring.

I think we sometimes forget because we don't care. Our hearts are these half-thawed, ho-hum entities that put out just enough to perpetuate their positions. Nothing more. If we truly care, we put ourselves on the line. We commit to the present. We work our way out of indifference and unwillingness to the point where giving ourselves is natural. We don't get mesmerized by the glamour then forget to bring our best consciousness to both the big and small tasks of our everyday lives. We are aware. We are alive.

We haven't forgotten a thing.

DIVINE DEEPENING
What prevents you from giving your conscious best
to everything entrusted to you?
How is this serving you and those around?

Can you part for a second
with all that mind chatter
and get to know yourself?

OH, TO BE OUT OF MY MIND

He's out of his mind is a cliché that's got it all wrong. He wishes he was out of his mind. He wishes he was free of the continual bombardment of thoughts that hound him from daybreak till bedtime, and on into dreamland.

Can you imagine one minute, how about a few seconds, when you could turn your mind off and not think about anything? Is it possible? Of course, we do it every day when we perform simple tasks. We are so focused, so given to something outside ourselves, we just don't notice our empty mind. Nevertheless, the stillness of mind is happening.

The craziest of us experience gaps in our mental chatter where peace and lucidity reign, and where the repetitive, reactive dialogue that defines us subsides and we are left with a sane mind whose only job is to cross the street with the flow of traffic . . . before the dump truck of the future backs right up to the tow truck of the past and trash talks our present into an unnoticed backdrop.

Therein lies the problem: We are too full of our incessant, time-based, thinking about the world and our business to be fully here. Our attention has been fractionated, infiltrated, hijacked and consumed to a point at which we are no longer aware of the beauty right in front of our noses. Quiet appreciation of life simply cannot compete with the thought bombardment streaming in our minds from the new president, the North Korea situation, health insurance premiums, on down to the big Hollywood divorce, not to mention our own relationship and survival issues.

Maybe that's why there are sporting events, sitcoms, and vacations. They allow our attention to pleasantly rest on the activity at hand. They stop us from obsessing over all the *what if's*. We get the breather we desperately need. But what happens when the popcorn's finished and the sandy beach has been left behind? It's time to fire up the old noggin to figure out life again. No, no, no, our renewed child protests: I just want to be back there and play. I want the joy of the breeze in the boat on the lake. I don't want the world.

What's the answer? Here are a few titles: *The Power of Now: A Guide to Spiritual Enlightenment* by Eckhart Tolle, *Be Here Now* by Ram Dass, and this ancient line, *Behold, now is the accepted time* from 2 Corinthians 6:2. In how many ways and by how many spiritual teachers must it be said: The only thing we have is

NOW. Either we are here or we are not. If we are not, then we are in our head. If we are in our head, how can we be conscious of the good at hand. Should we let something that will never get here, namely the past or the future, filibuster our lives. They have their place, of course, in the learning and planning process. Yet, they have no right (no real existence) to fill our heads with angst or aches nor to steal our peace.

In reality, each of us is the embodiment of presence as we text, talk, meet up with friends, and, yes, plan the future. I don't think it takes sitting under the Bodhi tree like the Buddha to embrace the eternal moment, or be embraced by it (nothing against this, I've invested years meditating to quiet my mind).

Will we ever get out of our minds? With consecrated practice, it's possible. Anything man sets himself to do, he can do. You want to run a marathon? Design a plan, put on shoes, and start grinding out the miles. After the side stitches and kinks are smoothed out, you'll probably experience runs where your mind seems like a steady stream of bliss and little else can interfere with you and that one act.

Years ago, while living in New York, I decided to learn meditation. My spiritual teacher showed me a way to focus my mind. I loved it. Yet, it was a constant struggle. I would drag the momentum of my city thoughts into class and spend the majority of the time running around in my head. I finally asked him what I should do. Begin quieting yourself down for however long it takes before you come, he suggested. That was a big request given the way I rushed around. I chose to commit myself to the discipline it took to become still and dispossessed of the craziness that ruled my mind. Within a few years, the quietness of mind that I sought became a reality.

I was, for the most part, *out of my mind* . . . and touching a peace I once thought impossible. What it takes each of us to reach this state will vary according to our temperament. But we can start right where we are, as we are. In other words, honestly accept ourselves: At this very moment, I am okay with the condition I am in. This helps remove the onus of battling a crazy mind. If it's that way, okay for now. I will persist. I will be easy on myself until the mind yields.

Watch. Allow. Focus.
Enjoy the Silence.

DIVINE DEEPENING

Isn't your peace of mind worth five minutes
upon waking and before sleeping?
Indulge in a mind-less break. Meditate.

If you are alone and lonely,
hug someone with your thought
and watch the blues go bye bye.

MR. LONELY

I don't wish it on anyone. Yet everyone with two legs and a heart seems to confront it one time or another. I've been afflicted with the it's-only-me-myself-and-I-and-the-four-walls blues real bad and wanted to hop the first plane outta here to the next life. Life had other plans for me, though, and twice refused my exit visa. "Earth for you, fella. Back to the dance." I would reluctantly obey and face another evening in my fourth-floor New York walk-up with the guy in the mirror.

Loneliness is the guy sitting on the sidelines at the dance. Loneliness is the little kid on a stoop with head hung as the neighborhood games whiz by. The world plays at their feet. They want to jump in, but making that one step is like crossing a vast frontier of questions and acceptance.

As grown-up kids, we keep the play going on as usual because we must. Our roles demand it. Besides, the world is watching and might think we have a problem and need help, which is as true as can be. Getting help would help. A kind word can go miles to bring us out of ourselves. But are we ready to receive one? Are we claiming our kinship with all life? If yes, the lonely

MARK LECLAIR DEGANGE

days are over; we are back in life's embrace. If not, we have allowed Mr. Lonely to claim the best part of us.

Why do you think booze, bars, and late night television were created?

If we're clever enough to dream up a depraved state called loneliness, why not un-dream it? We can see it as a momentary delusion, nothing too serious, and let it drift away without any fanfare into the far reaches of mental space where it's at best a vague memory. Out goes another mask with the garbage; in comes the smile of a new day.

I forgot one thing: The banished quality I call Mr. Lonely sure as heck does not like his name or nature. The only way he can even be is if he attaches himself to some sad sack. So, he heads straight back to the only home he ever knew, you. He sees the new paint job on the front door of your heart and hesitates, but only for a second. He's not fooled by the paint. He knows that nothing has changed inside.

He doesn't bother to knock; he simply slides his cool, droopy self in, slips into pajamas, slinks forward and settles comfortably in the corner of the couch to get ready for the late-night murder movie. *Beer and chips, please.*

64

Let's turn this picture off. Who wants a rerun.

It's not easy to switch the channel. Our unwanted guest has a mind of his own, and a will to match. He insists on following you around, no, not exactly following, but clinging to you like clammy sweat from a workout. He doesn't stop there. He enjoys having things his way. If you get a sudden itch to see a friend or share more of yourself, he quickly wells up a wad of self-pity and attempts to overrule you before plans can germinate. Soon he's even dictating the somber pace you walk, and the way you talk, which lately has become filled with pauses and somber tones, and sentences laying half-spoken and half-dead in your mouth. He tops it off with the lack of care you put into your cooking—it's only for you anyway, so why bother to make it special.

He's got you. The curtains are drawn; the walls have utterly nothing to say; the kitchen clock reminds you of the end of another day. Worst of all, he wants the best room of the house, your heart space, as his private bedroom. *Good night.*

I'm getting pretty fed up thinking about this shiftless leech, this tyrant, who's so self-centered that he has the nerve to flop down wherever he pleases and squelch any joy that comes your way.

How do you kick this little tyrant out for good?

The quick way is to know he never was a part of you, just a figment of the dream of self-pity. That may be too tall an order. Then what to do?

Here's a plan. It's a bit sly, and that's why I think it will work—it meets him at his own game and one-ups him.

Sit on your couch in a very lazy, enervated posture. Purposely have no positive thoughts. Feel down and lonely. In other words, accept the way things are. He will absolutely love it and be as unconscious and deadbeat as ever. Now don't pour the depression on too, too heavy. He doesn't go in for drama; he fears it could lead to a telephone call for help. Just sink into the couch with a few mildly self-deprecating thoughts and he won't suspect a thing.

Very slowly, without making much effort (remember, he loathes effort), sit up straight. He might object at first to the posture. Just don't add alertness to the posture. He'll let it pass. Take a weak inhalation through the mouth and let it out with a sigh. He'll think you are sighing out of your why-bother-with-life attitude. (This gives him a perverse sense of happiness.) Take another breath, this time through the nose, and bring it deep into your heart. He's used to shallow breaths and the deep breath will catch him off guard and make him dizzy and not quite aware of what he is doing in your heart in the first place. Exhale with a deliberate, good riddance sigh. He'll feel as if part of him has been sucked away. He's right; it has.

Before he can react, throw another deep breath right into the center of your heart and picture a great sun, a super nova even, exploding like the Fourth of July in your chest. Feel his gloomy morale shatter. Hold the breath and feel the pressure of it. Bounce him out of any corners he may be hiding. Don't let up on him. Pin him down and watch the luminosity of the sun's warmth dissolve any vestiges of him. Exhale a sigh of relief. Check to see if his stagnant, depressed self is anywhere. If so, repeat the deep breaths, expanding sun, vigorous exhale thing a number of times with conviction. Know that you are taking your life back.

Now stand up. Stretch your limbs. Shake your hands, arms, legs, and feet. Feel as if you are flicking off gobs of tension. You are. In fact, it is the stiff remnants of Mr. Lonely. Any healthy movements are anathema to him—remember this. If you still feel weighted down, go outside and run, jump, or climb a tree and get a liberating view. Make the air and the ground your friends. Feel like you belong to life.

Give the first person you see a big "Hello."

A house full of joy has no room for a Mr. Lonely. Be advised, though, at the first sign of tail-spinning "woe is me," the door opens for this shiftless squatter to come take up residence.

Our job is to stay in the dance. To reach out. To keep the door to our heart swinging both ways. Then, whether we are with others or not, the sun will still play on our bedroom walls and a big smile will play in our heart.

DIVINE DEEPENING

Are you ready to embrace that loneliness
out of existence?
Say "Yes," and disprove it was ever a real part of you.
Use the fun method in the article if you
need more help.

The past is outdated, outlawed time.
The future is unknown, untouched time.
The present is forever now. I'm in.

WHY KOWTOW TO A NUMBER

Being on the brink of another birthday I wonder, why must I age? What is aging anyway? A larger number tagged onto me defining a stage of life? More cells dying than cells being reborn? Telomeres shortening? Limbs stiffening? Senses shutting down? Being slower and more tired? Yuck.

I haven't asked gerontologists, nor have I sought out the wisdom of centenarians. I have other things to do. Somehow, the idea of aging strikes me as wholly missing the point of living and making now the only life. Why be a captive of time?

Getting Old. These words are a bugaboo for our time-conscious world, and an excuse to slow down and stop. They remind me of a TV cartoon train engine with a droopy metal face that's been lugging its heavy iron body around forever. As it chugs into the station, each exasperated huff and puff of smoke is a medley of "Can't do it, anymore; Can't do it, gettin' old; Can't do it, gonna stop." If life is about dragging a tired body over hill and dale, then I'll stay parked in the station, please.

As maturing has been portrayed—I've-made-up-my-mind mentalities congealing into settled bodies—I will never go for. No one has a right to damn the spring in your step no matter how much they profess about life.

In my teens and twenties (there I go being time-defined), I had a few careers and a host of odd jobs. I wasn't satisfied. I was restless, always searching for the right feeling, the best way for me. Though I was clear enough to know what I didn't want: jobs offering mediocre satisfaction that grind down your spirit into a disgruntled shuffle and lease you two to four weeks a year and a paltry pension after forty or so laps around the sun. Top off this nonlife in your favorite chair glued to the latest reality thriller radiating from the flat screen.

I could have puked. But I didn't wait to get to the main course. I hopped on my horse and charged away to live. I wasn't one hundred percent sure how or where I was headed. But, I trusted my heart to lead.

The horse got a nonstop workout trying to chase my heart. I'm surprised the horse didn't stop at the nearest water hole and call it quits. I suspect that it, too, would have gotten restless. The ride was what it was all about. So, hitching across the United States became the next thing; playing Olympic sports and attending Olympic Games had their day; traveling to faraway lands I almost became one of their own; launching a theater career in New York cast its spell; calling my soulmate to me and voyaging together had its time too; and then I turned inward to discover the universe.

Along the way, I became convinced I could retard the aging process. My horse gave a groan not knowing which way to go. I did. We lurched forward into the rounds of beguiling bookstores, seeking seers, chewing Chinese roots, cleansing colon therapy, anti-oxidants, audiences with Ramtha the enlightened one, Tibetan exercises, meditation, pyramid sitting and more. I was gung-ho for the eternal noon.

I believed, and still do. Though I've relaxed my live-to-127-or-bust program. My life has retained a few of the outward disciplines though more of the inner consecration. I find calm innards a more reliable health ticket. A more peaceful psyche has softened the intensity of my quests.

And being 40, 50, and beyond, what's that? Bigger numbers, yes. Ideas of myself I am reacting to by writing this piece, most likely. Maybe ages are only reminders from the Universe how precious life is.

Why should I give a hoot about being an adult. An adult is only a child in a bigger body who plays at knowing something. Have I found the right answers to stay bouncy and youthful? They will probably change as I change. What I practice most is being present, so as not to miss out on the joy at hand.

Life's possibilities beckon. The only sensible course is to keep jumping in and discovering. Nurturing the next, best, on-the-plate ideas, and see where they take me, and whatever else is waiting in the well of creation. Time will step aside and wave me by as the rejuvenating spring inside feels too good to stop.

DIVINE DEEPENING

Are the countless, creative possibilities lurking
inside you getting out to play? Whatever you answer,
choose the one thing your heart has put
on the back burner
and let it be the horse that now carries you forward.

MEDITATION

Conscious Care

This meditation is about being present. It is a step in being conscious and focused wherever you are and in whatever you are doing. Let's begin. Conscious care starts right where you choose to meditate today--the chair, the couch, the special rug. Get comfortable. Get present by yielding your body to the support of the furniture, the spot, etc. Be aware of the air as a life-support system touching and lovingly molding itself to every part of you. Breathe in this life support. Consciously exhale as if your breathing out is nurturing the air and everything around you. Do this a few times.

How is your heart? Does it feel alive? Is it open? Ask for more love and more aliveness. Ask your heart to open to this moment. Keep asking until you feel it open.

Gratitude. What aspect of your life needs more gratitude? More appreciation? More of your love? More you? You know. Let the answer come into your mind. See how you treat this part of your life. Please don't berate yourself. Simply notice.

Now is the time to choose to care. Internally say: *I am opening my heart to* . . . (that aspect of your life) now and forever (Know that you are actually doing this. Your decree has power.) *I am bringing my best and only self to this. I honestly am. I am releasing all resistance to* . . . *I am at one with myself and* . . . (If you sense you need more completion, then repeat the words with more commitment until you feel satisfied.) If something or someone else comes up that needs your conscious care, then begin again, *I am opening my heart to* . . .

Be aware of your thoughts and emotions and how you now feel about whatever you chose to master. Be aware if there is still any inharmonious feeling inside. Breathe in and exhale with a relaxed "ahhh." Feel yourself yielding. Feel the resistance melt out of you. Do you feel one with your chosen object of attention? Do you feel totally at ease with it? Sit with it. Embrace it. Incorporate it into you.

Then let it all go. Be conscious of your heart and how caring it is. Remember to take it with you wherever you go, whatever you do.

3

CHAPTER

SOUL OFFERINGS

Do your heart's leadings make you feel
Heavy and mired?
Drop 'em and don't look back.
But if they make you feel
Light and lifted
Follow them till they play out.

ASCENDING ARC

I am cherishing the ascending arc
Of the eagle's flight
How it soars and sings
Into breathtaking freedom.

Its soaring is not an option
It's a must.

I, too, cast my sights on high—
My heart has played its hand in heaven
And it's a full house of good
I should have known
Life could give me no less.

It is not fate
Dealt to chosen ones (we all are chosen)
But the way it is
In the openly secret place
Where the sun has no bounds
And the infinite blue goodness of eternity
Draws all eyes and lifts all hearts.

DIVINE DEEPENING

Picture your life soaring into the heights
of freedom of self-expression.
Then write, sing, draw how that would be.
Savor your creation as a declaration to live by.

SOUL OFFERINGS

Either I care, and do
or I don't care, and don't do.

THE POINT

The point is

To feel and never stop allowing the gamut
Of humanity's trials and triumphs
To touch my being in some meaningful way to elicit
My compassion, my kindness, my caring and
My bravos.

Why do I have a heart if not to remember
An absent loved one, to encourage a struggling
Friend, and to help a burdened neighbor?
Every smile shared, every selfless act rendered,
Expands the very pith of my heart.

You, Beloved, have given me this living heart
To reach out to your creation,
To partake in its beauty,
And to be awed by its presence
in my life.

You are too generous. My arms fill quickly
With all the gifts of goodness to be given.

Then I rest and give thanks.
For another day has expanded my life with a host
Of new reasons to offer myself and
The highest feelings I can muster to You
And all the dear ones You share with me.

DIVINE DEEPENING

A toughie—In what chamber of your heart don't you care enough? Are you willing to put your heart on the line? Practical steps, please.

Love's healing voice—
I live for no other.

THIS VOICE

Where did this voice come from?
insistent
wrenching
persistent

        need I must live with

With my voice
I give You
My all
     whatever
         I am

Know that my wail shall not cease
Until my body and soul are yours.

I will sing
The guttural
Like a Flamenco *cantaor*
Whose only solace
Is to lay his psyche bare
In the street

And maybe, when my passion is used up,
I'll know where this voice came from

Thank you
For driving me
From continent to continent
Through lives, loves, and
Myriad obsessions that strove
To be my life
And now feel like
Fantasy fallen away

What have I gained?
Will a few drops of peace
Seduce my voice?
Do a few drops of honey in the hive
Stop the bees' work?

You, my Love,
Have planted this voice
Within
I want to know
Its full use—
Give me the Word!

But I am patient
I won't burst
Before my heart fully speaks.

DIVINE DEEPENING

Are you honoring your true voice?
What would that look like? If that voice
is presently pained and/or angry, are you
still willing to honor it?

Are you in the way, yourself,

or in the way of Self?

A TRAIL OF YOUR GLORY

Let the days of my life be filled with your
Abundant graces.
Let me not miss a moment to commit myself to You
In the highest way possible. When I fall, fail, or
Simply forget, please wake me and right me, quickly,
So I may go in the way You are leading and leave
A trail marked by your glory.

I know I am an infinitesimally tiny part of your plan,
Of your sweeping majesty.
I can only laugh when I rise up in my grandeur
Thinking how splendid I am. Yes, I truly am
A wonder when your light lightens my soul.
But the frame, the deed, the money, the fame,
They're yours—let them declare You.

I'll fulfill the roles and responsibilities
You've entrusted to me
and hopefully be about them with a smile.
Then, when the life of my desires is spent like a
Dissolving day, I'll still be left with the space of You.
Even this prayer is a desire I must let go of—and I do.

DIVINE DEEPENING

If your answer to the question on p. 92
is yourself, then what adjustments
to your working ethos need to be made?

SOUL OFFERINGS

When the sun is directly overhead
there's no shadow.
When Soul is the only guide
there's no shadow of a doubt.

THE GROVE

Lately, I've called
Out to You
My ever Friend
Do you hear me?

Do You have a room ready
A fresh, bright, spacious one
With windows opening on forever?
Is the door with my name
In place?

I know I am anxious
Restless . . . Yet I am given
Won't you send a sign?
Watch and Wait and Work and Wait

Why do You hide?

How can I lure You into the open?
What forgotten words can I offer You?
Tell me where—in what dried-up river bed—
Do they lie?
That I may go the dusty path
By miles of starlight, and there
On my hands and knees
                    dig them up for You.

If I shout my demand
Even throw a thunderbolt
From my throat
Off the highest peak
That shakes the very fabric of the sky

What then . . .
Would You show yourself?

I ask You for a sign
Nothing
not even a glimpse.

The play feels old
The stage littered
With a life, mine
Actors
Costumes
Shoes
Props
                          scattered about
I long
        to lay down
        everything
From the grandiose statements
To the least noticed breath
To walk off barefoot
Humming, and join You in the wings
Where the play really begins.

I sound young; they say
Thirty-five, maybe forty—
Inwardly I used to gloat
Ah, I will live to 127
And be ageless and wise . . .
And rest on a line
In a book of records.
If tomorrow was the day
I'd gladly give away
Every one of those years to
Whomever wants them

To be with You,
My Beloved,
Who patiently feeds
And watches, while I
Reckon with business
Here.

What to do
With this feeling
Toss it?
Give it back to You?
I'd be lost
My life impossible

You are the Soul
Within all passions

The heart's cry to be home

I am realistic
My time hasn't come
The play is on and
I have my part:
        I will make the room
        Prepare the altar
        And carry its sunlight in my arms
        Through the shadowy grove
        To keep the way well lit.

DIVINE DEEPENING

How are you heeding your soul's yearning
for that which really feeds you?

Heaven is a choice
and I choose it now.

WHAT MY LIFE WOULD LOOK LIKE

My life as a heavenly blessing,
What would it look like?

Would unspeakable peace mark my presence?
Would it be impossible to speak but in praises?
Would deaf ears perk up when I sing?
Would I act as a perfect partner with the day?
Would I move like a caressing breeze thru the crowd?
Would I be a gentle refrain to my harshest critic?
Would I see through my tormentor to the good?
Would a fearful child come and play next to me?
Would discomfort's edges find ease in me?
Would I inspire a sad soul out of itself?
Would I be a home to those gone astray?
Would my hands touch the untouchable?

I pray so.

DIVINE DEEPENING
What heaven on earth are you not choosing?

MEDITATION

Soul Expression

Go to your favorite place in nature where you have privacy. Or create a favorite place. This is your power spot. Get into a comfortable, well-supported sitting position. Be there at your favorite time of day. Breathe naturally. Let your body and your entire being melt into the environment, as if this setting was designed for you. It was. As you breathe, let any tension, any un-you, unwind on the exhalations. Keep your eyes are open.

Feel the joy of being there and soaking in every bit of nature through your senses. Feel the joy of being yourself. Feel aliveness resonate through you. Feel so present, so full of being, that your oneness fills up the entire vista before you. It's as if the beautiful, peaceful environment spread before you is coming out of you, and is you. Take your time. Relish and hold this expanded state of being for as long as you desire. You have everything you need. You are one with nature. You are one with yourself. Your soul is in its native element of union.

Now close your eyes. Take this feeling of oneness within and without into any field of expression you desire, be it work, play, relationships, etc. See how fully yourself you are and how expanded you feel in that area of your life just by sharing your current state. Taste it. Flourish in it. Be it. If any resistance appears, be easy with this, too. The key is not opposition, but acceptance. There is no need to change anything. Accept. Melt. Share. Accept, melt, share, and be one.

When ready, stand up and be aware of yourself in this sacred space. Know that you can recreate this full expression of soul wherever you are and transform your world.

4
CHAPTER

AWESOME YOU

*The germ of every right aught
rests complete in Godly thought.*

MORNING LISTENING PRELUDE

Infinitude speaks in
Glorified tones of silence
Trumpeted forth from on high

Listen and rejoice:

"Be as I am, and so
Be perfectly as you are—
It is royally enough for Me
And my creation."

Now go bound forward in
Your song of grace
Let your colors ascend
To the applause of angels.

DIVINE DEEPENING
Listen, and in the silence of self-acceptance
let your soul speak its glory.

WARNING: *The pattern, tradition, or script you are enacting— the world's, your family's, your friends', an organization's— could be destructive to your well-being. Feel free to toss it and be the thespian of your heart.*

PERMISSION TO BE

We must give ourselves permission *to be*. No one else can. Who can allow us, but us? We are the door that opens to our deepest, truest self. We are the ones opening it, too.

I'm sure you know all this. So why say it? Because not walking through the door costs us our lives. I saw it up close growing up, and it was painful to watch. One of my dad's two passions was cooking food—which I mention in the Q&A. His food blessed many people. But what he not-so-secretly wanted was to be a professional cook, even have his own restaurant. At the dinner table some evenings he would ask us kids, "How much do you think I could charge for this?" We would cringe as he suggested a few prices. Isn't it way better to let fly our heart of hearts and wherever it lands so be it? Getting our statement out in the world could nudge open others' doors as well. Since I love words, saying it is one of my ways of walking through the door.

Unless I give voice to what's cookin' in my heart, the spirit in me languishes, ruminates, diverts, constipates, short-circuits, and, eventually dies, instead of leaping into the open. When the spirit in me isn't let out, I become like one of those penny arcade pinball machines whose metal balls (my thoughts and desires) ricochet, colliding with my own actions, bouncing off possibilities, getting shunted in paths unwanted and then hurling towards the flippers (my flailing self). I miss, of course, and the ball drops out of sight into the darkness of my mind's underbelly. Game over.

Ugh, this can't be me. Truthfully, it's not. So what sad rerun about myself am I mucking around in that could possibly stop me from being the real me?

It's too easy to blame my parents, background, education, and circumstance. My past has its share of hiccups, disappointments, and false starts. But, it's done and gone. Why hold on to it as if it has something to offer? Why talk to all my friends so earnestly about my trials and suffering? Dysfunctional histories are not uplifting unless the moral of the story is to rise above them. I can keep reacting to them, or stop telling them.

What really stops me? What keeps the door to my heart closed? Unworthiness, with its life-damning executioner named *condemnation*. If I wield its sword, there goes life. The joyful child in me gets his hopes quashed, his heart sealed, and his life sentenced to inner Siberia.

It's a royal injustice to think I am worth less than I am. I am lying to myself without knowing it. My value is inestimable. In itself my life (anyone's life) without lifting a finger is so bountiful in qualities, ideas, and creativity that anything is possible. My job is to know I have what it takes to fulfill these amazing possibilities of me. Who could be me, and say my story like me? No one in the universe. My being is necessary. The universe needs me for it to be complete. I walk and talk, laugh and cry, dance and sing, and yes, stumble and get up, like no other being that ever was.

Don't wait, it's time to play. Charge your inner turbo. Flash the green light. Run out the door, and go for it.

DIVINE DEEPENING
Are you posing as someone else? Are you basing life on something outside of you?
Expose this to your heart's true desire. No contest.

*I never met an individual who isn't
the greatest story ever told.
Soul couldn't be less.*

WELCOME GENA

Early Saturday morning. That's a good excuse to sleep in. Besides, I need an occasional breather. I'm too caught up in the New York, New York can't-do-without-yo-act syndrome.

We need blue laws here. No joke. Set aside one day in which everything closes. We'll call it, *Island Retreat Day.* No business. No cabs. No theater. No Times Square lights. Nada.

It won't happen today, though. The clock is rapidly telling me I will be late for meditation if I don't hurry my legs out of here. I whip out the door, through the streets and come flying off the elevator into the coatroom, unloading coat, shoes, and heaving heart in one beat. At this rate, I'll need the meditation to get over the effects of getting in the door.

Come straightway to the river and plunge in and let the current take you is the unspoken message in my heart as I look at Gena, the meditation teacher, who has metamorphosed from a Brooklyn mother of two to a Native American sage.

I trust her. She is an old, old friend. We have been on this journey before. I surrender completely. Our eyes and our senses recede. I like dissolving. I am engulfed in a field of light that gets stronger as the play of our souls deepens and accelerates in a spiral of brilliance and pervasiveness like a Mongolian sun that drenches and bathes us until we are breathing the still, silent power of Mind.

I am not Mark. She is not Gena. We have gone through a veil; we swim in a new language of pure energy. I know I am conscious. I am sitting on a wooden floor. I feel a vibrant energy in my body. It's like the Fourth of July inside me. Molten balls shoot up my spine and burst in my brain, spraying streams of living chills in every direction. Not stopping there, the electricity cascades downward and exclaims *Wow* in my chest and *Ooo* in my belly. My legs and feet are touched by a shimmering vibration too.

With one shamanistic wave of her hand, Gena is gone. I work to hold the concentrated state but the energy seems to dissipate. I feel alone. It's time to dig in and allow those fires of focus to continue.

Class ends. After the customary hugs, Gena walks over smiling. Another hug. Jana is the epitome of simplicity: Here's my heart, want some? She is so unpretentious, like a child taking everything in for the first time. Ready to learn. Willing to do. Whether she is scrubbing floors or watering plants, she gives of her-self without expectation. She seems to gravitate to the dirty, unglamorous jobs. She reminds me of a sturdy, old Ukrainian woman on 9th Street who I see sweeping the sidewalk and tidying up the garbage barrels.

Gena, you always do *these* jobs. What about jobs that thrust you into the limelight where you have the power and run the show—are you hiding from those? Your fear of heights seems a metaphor for you not standing out.

I sense that the time is coming for you to make a move. To leap into newness and proclaim, I am capable of . . . . To dust yourself off. Don the street smart dress of this age and see your life click right along with the pace of a New York day. You might surprise yourself. I won't be surprised. I'll just heartily applaud you, sister.

DIVINE DEEPENING
What thought change, what heart reset, is necessary for you to stop dimming your light and actually step into it?

What are you missing?

Aren't you here?

INCOMPARABLE YOU

Comparisons are deadly. They steal your heart. They elevate someone at your expense, and leave you in a self-exiled backroom of envy, lack, and "I'll-never-amount-to . . . or accomplish-that" mind trips.

Having danced with this I can tell you, it wastes your time and your life. On top of it, it's unreasonable, impossible, and downright unfair to compare yourself with another. They fill their niche and you yours. Would you want anyone to put you above them, and deprive themselves of their own life?

Chalk up another murdered heart.

You are irreplaceable, irreproducible, and forever the one and only you walking the earth. Believe this with your whole heart. Every single one of us has purpose and destiny that can't be filled by another. From the special circumstances of your growing up to your idiosyncratic mannerisms to your highs, your lows, the light in your eyes, and on and on and on—it's all and only you. Who thinks like you? Cares like you? Wails in joy when your all-time favorite song plays? No one, but you.

Why then would anyone want to covet your life, measure themselves against you, or vice versa, when theirs is equally special, beautiful, quirky, holy, and ultimately indecipherable?

What Spirit did in creating you was a first take. Done perfectly special, too—the crux of this diatribe. "You're a shining star"—as the R&B music group Earth, Wind, and Fire once put it. You need only take stock of that joyful fact. Taking stock of anything less leaves you at the back of the bus, not in the driver's seat.

The world loves to hold up superstars. Let them be. Where does putting them on a pedestal leave me? Nowhere, if they are Olympic athletes and I am just a good runner who will never make the Games; nowhere, if they are Broadway icons and I am an unknown actor building my resume; nowhere, if they are mighty healers, saints, and I am an occasional healer who strives to trust his own heart.

Give bravos where they are due, especially if some-one is making a contribution to this world. I totally respect that. Appreciating quality shows our quality. We are elevated.

But playing a comparing game really puts you on the bench. If Joe Hero scores a thousand points while I miss two crucial free throws what do I do? Give less effort and think, Joe will do it for me. Then my play goes down and I do worse. Have I forgotten all I bring to the game? Look at Lebron James losing the ball a number of times in the closing minutes of a 2013 NBA championship game before teammate Ray Allen beau-tifully drilled the game winner as time ran out. Did Lebron bury himself because of his ball-hogging mis-takes? No. I doubt he felt good about his play; but he shook it off (didn't allow it to define him) and went on to be named series MVP. Three years later his unstop-pable play brought down the mighty Warriors in the NBA Finals and again he became MVP. If he had dwelt on not being the great Michael Jordan could he have done what he did?

Comparing ourselves with another's accomplishments get us nowhere and delays our living on the level of those we aspire to be like. A few sense their missions early on and are quick out of the gate. Be grateful for their example and let them be. You have no idea, though, what's really going on with them—their sacrifice, their suffering, even their self-esteem quotient. The greatest Olympic gold medalist of all time, the swimmer Michael Phelps, was in the pits of low self-worth and despair between the London and Rio Olympics. How many gold medals does it take?

None. Be the gold medalist of your heart. And let it shine.

DIVINE DEEPENING

Isn't it exhausting trying to
measure up to someone else?
You never get there.
Stop trying. Be your own measure.

Are you a desert
that no one wants to cross
or an oasis
where all love to drink?

HAVE YOU NOTICED

Take a look, and observe
What a lovely creation you are
It's not ego; it's a fact
Being you

A zillion flawlessly formed phrases
Beaming like rays of the sun and
Brimming with the beatitudes of a baby
Could never capture
Your once-in-an-eternity suchness

Have you noticed

Have you stopped today
And let life kiss you all over

Have you let your soul's smile out
To play with the birds and the breezes

Have you opened the treasury
Of your cherished feelings
And lofted them on high

Have you let another
Bathe in your holy temple

If you haven't, perhaps
Now is the time.

DIVINE DEEPENING
Why hoard your gold?
Share it, and more will appear.

MEDITATION

The Greatest Story Ever Told

I am. I am. I truly am . . . the most beautiful, gifted, and valued individual ever known, as is every other person who has ever lived. Indeed, you are like royalty from on high come to grace this earth.

So please sit upright in your chair like the king or queen you are. Allow your body to fill the space with peace, poise, and power. Feet are planted firmly on floor. Hands folded on your lap right by your navel. This is your sovereign time. Close your eyes. Take three conscious breaths with the following intentions:

1) Imagine the I AM in you waking up infinite love and exhaling all vestiges of fear
2) Imagine the I AM in you waking up infinite intelligence and exhaling any sense of ignorance
3) Imagine the I AM in you waking up infinite power and wealth and exhaling all weakness and lack

Fully claim the love, wisdom, and power of the I AM.

Now place your attention about two finger widths below the navel. This is your center of power and balance. Let every breath drop into the well there. Feel the energy expand. See the light grow there. Imagine you have a mega-kilowatt generator of power and creativity in your navel area. Enjoy a deep, sated sense of well-being there. Imagine you live in a mighty ocean of belly bliss.

Move your attention to the center of your forehead, your seat of vision. Imagine you have a portal of light there. Know your center of balance below supports your vision center. Let the light grow brighter and more radiant in your third eye. Feel yourself expand into the light there. Ask for a clearer vision of your life. Surrender yourself into the light. Know that the clear light is your vision and destiny and it is actualized now.

Then move into the heart center. Take a breath into the center of your chest and feel your heart open. Your heart is like a pure white flower whose petals welcome your mind's holy intent. Feel the beauty of your spirit there. Let a magnificent sacred light unfold—your immortal individuality—the essence of I AM. See the I AM (your true power) spread from your heart through a central channel of light within, uniting your navel and third eye centers and then filling your entire body. Acknowledge your beautiful temple of wisdom, power and love. Dwell for a few minutes in the perfect union of these three aspects of your divinity.

Wrap up the meditation with gratitude for the unique gift of life that you have to share with this world.

BEHOLD

5

CHAPTER

THE HEART
OF IT ALL

Love is soft, and flows easily.
Hate is hard, and takes energy.

LOVE ONE ANOTHER

The final guideline given by the Master Teacher was "Love one another." To me this is the highest, most complete, and simplest statement of human ethics ever uttered, and it was a clear directive not some dreamy platitude of life on earth that couldn't be fulfilled.

Think about it: **Love** is the first word. The Holy of Holies. It initiates and is the principle of all conscious action. It has the authority to harmoniously connect **one** with **another,** and to maintain that oneness. Love can be thought of as the indissoluble, universal glue forever holding everything in place, in which no evil intent can enter to separate.

When we put *love* first, *one another* flows naturally together from it. Check it out on the following page:

Smelling a newborn's pure head
      Welcoming the wayward boy
Forgiving the attacker
      Giving your sandwich to the curbside sitter
Sharing the best part
      Consoling the grieving heart
Nursing the suffering child
      Offering a heart (not an eye) for an eye
Allowing another to go ahead
      Going out of your way
Letting them know they are worth it
      Lending an ear when there's nothing in it
      for you
Playing to the good in the face of their attitude
      Loving them, despite no common ground,
      even dislike
Reaching out your hand in truce

DIVINE DEEPENING

To whom do you need to reach out to
fulfill your highest destiny to love?
Decide what the act will be.

If I am so intent on what is right
for someone, am I sure
I haven't already lost them?

HUGS, NOT HEADS

"All I wanted was a hug." Ugh, I felt horrible. How could I have missed that badly. I stood there at a loss for words. I was like a boxer who just got tagged. My heart was reeling. She sat there on the carpet leaning against the wall hurting—and waiting for me. Not pointing the finger, just clearly expressing her need. I finally got over the ringing of her words in my ears (and in my ego) and went to over to her and hugged her and expressed remorse for having overlooked her needs.

This may not sound like a big thing, but it was for me. Here I was the budding healer/therapist thinking I was on my game. I had divined what my girlfriend needed with my oriental diagnostic tools. I was in control and would wisely pronounce the nature of her imbalance and its remedy—Yes, in the cool abstraction of my head, which had nothing to do with her heart, or mine.

What does a crying baby need when it's fearful? A doctor's questions and finger probes or the immediacy of its mother's hug? It's no contest: Love is balm for every wail and wound. In my shiatsu training, nurturing had been emphasized as the main approach to touch, not analysis. When you nurture the part of a person that is deficient (a yin, weak state), energy will often flow from the excessive area (a yang, defended state). There's no judgment involved. It's a matter of listening and being where the need is.

I am constantly reminded in my own family to listen with care first. The suggestions can come after. Who doesn't feel better when they know the person(s) closest to them are right there with ears and hugs. I wasn't raised in a huggy family, so I had to work on that one. The temptation is to rush in and save with wordy gems of experience. They have their place. But they ain't first responders. Maybe a close second if couched in kindness and/or a loving touch.

Especially as a parent it's so easy to fall into thinking, *I've been through it all. I know. Here is the solution that you* (my son or daughter) *should see, take to heart, and now act with to get past your issue—take it from me.*

Kiss that opportunity for closeness goodbye. Children sense right away if you are there for them or doing your blowhard, know-it-all crap. They'll let you know, too, now, or much later when it's safer, and hopefully not too late. Shutting your mouth and being fully present is often enough to give them exactly what they want.

My Superdad, I'll-save-you, cape was trashed long ago. My frank children made sure of that.

Wouldn't it be a relief not to feel pressured to figure anyone out? Can I really divine what is best for someone other than me, even if they are my family? Maybe. Often it smacks of controlling and not trusting that their own heart can do the job. I like what the ascended master Ramtha said years ago when asked by a parent how they should teach their children: "When they ask."

I think that applies nicely for most relationships. When in doubt, just listen and be ready with a hug.

DIVINE DEEPENING
Listen to others, it will change you.
The next person you run across listen to
with every fiber of your being and see.

*Find one thing you love in someone
and watch it beautify their whole story.*

APPLYING GANDHI TO A FAULT

I couldn't tolerate this guy. I had to admit it. I couldn't avoid him either. We lived on the same floor in the same small, college dorm. I never considered myself more likable than him. Nor did I dislike him because of the motor-mouthed way he and his two New York buddies parodied everything under the sun. The parodies seemed harmless—actually loads of fun—and a raucous window into how New York captures the minds and hearts of its native sons and then through them spews out its psyche over everything in a New Yorker's path.

New York or not, these were college guys, not saints. What could I expect?

The rub was, his two friends had innocence in their play; he had a me-me-me-centeredness. It felt as if he didn't care for anything or anyone except what came out of his mouth. This fueled my growing repulsion. Was I envious? Not really. I saw nothing in him that I aspired to. Nevertheless I was rubbed wrong by this guy, and didn't know what to do about it.

The one thing I imagined that would satisfy my loathing of him was wailing away on him in a good fight—as if a solid punch would relieve me of my distaste for this guy or make him less selfish.

What opened the door to healing was eventually realizing what I was feeling was squarely in me, and up to me, to sort out. No need going to him. I needed to straighten myself out. In those days, I didn't have a male friend or mentor I trusted enough to confide in—nor any kind of spiritual life to fall back on.

I had recently begun studying philosophy. The contemplation of man's nature had had a quieting effect on me. My normal approach to life had been action. I would physicalize any angst felt, which often resulted in destruction to my body and objects in my path. Now I was learning to step back and contemplate, and not let passion have the whole say.

One of my discoveries was Gandhi. His philosophy of nonviolence resonated in me. Standing up peacefully to selfishness, injustice, whatever, without fighting seemed a much better way to gain my own heart besides my fellow brother's ear. In particular, Gandhi's insistence on seeing the light within another got me thinking: Why couldn't I apply this to the issue I was having with my dorm mate.

I didn't really see the light in this guy; I wasn't sure what that was supposed to look like. I decided to focus on something about him I could like. I latched onto it and did my best to relate to him through it. Slowly I felt a softening towards him. A sense of goodwill, I'll call it, spread in my thought until I was no longer bothered by him. Maybe I was seeing the light.

I even imagined I enjoyed his self-absorbed attitude.

We never became fast friends. Though we did play together on the flag football team that won the college championship. More importantly, it was a huge step in getting past myself to see the light in another.

DIVINE DEEPENING
Pick a person that you have had trouble with. Can you find something in them to relate to and like? Persist, persevere, and watch your friendship grow.

When your heart is not in it
you are not in it.

THE ART IS IN THE HEART

Have you ever practiced an art, a sport—some discipline—with fervor and intelligence, knowing it was your thing, then some rookie comes along and executes as naturally and beautifully the first time as if they were born doing it? That can set you on your heels and/or leave you in awe.

One crisp winter morning I headed west on East 9th Street in New York on my way to the Upper West Side for an acting class in the Ansonia Hotel. I crossed Second Avenue at a fast clip minding my own business. As I approached a driveway leading into a car repair shop I saw a large man with an old Army coat standing there. It would have been easy to assign him "bum status" and rush on by. It was cold, too.

He had just bitten into an oversized Milky Way bar and was chewing with a deep, satisfied look of enjoyment on his face. I came next to him to pass, and he looked down (he towered over me) and said, "Mmmm Goood!" with such a forceful and joyful conviction that the air seemed to resonate with his happiness.

I lit up with a smile. This early in the day, what could top that? His exclamation of pure pleasure was blazed in my memory forever.

At the time, I also was taking commercial acting classes at Weist-Barron's, and learning how to project. There he was, probably homeless and untutored, yet so naturally bringing to life what we actors strive to create, an animated sense of reality. How? His heart was totally in it.

One take and it was a wrap. I was in awe—lifted, humbled, and utterly convinced.

DIVINE DEEPENING

Are you busy impressing
and divorced from being?

Is life feasting on you
or eating you alive?

STARVING AT THE FEAST

Flowers bend toward and open to the sun. They don't hide or cower. They naturally lean in. Birds ride the air currents across the skies. Can you imagine if they decided to fold up their wings in midflight? Disastrous! They gracefully allow those currents to carry them. Large whales open their mouths and take in huge quantities of small fish and microorganisms. Could they survive if they didn't open their mouths? Nature shows how every living thing uniquely receives what it needs for its existence.

Being able to receive opens the door to the universe. Scientists were receptive to the physics of space flight in enabling men to go to the moon and back. Otherwise, an *ain't-a-possibility* mindset would have kept man bound to Earth.

People unwilling to receive often will say, "I'm okay," "I can do it," or "Don't worry, I'll take care of it."—as they angle you away from helping. It could be your time to receive, and do nothing. If you resist and insist on helping them, then it could be your issue, too. Self-sufficiency is great. Completing a project by yourself can feel fantastic—and it may free another to do what they love. How much easier life would be, though, if you allow someone to lend a helping hand.

What stops us from receiving? We all have our own reasons. A few of mine have been unworthiness, pride and inadequacy. Too much self, of one kind or another, can shut us down. We would rather suffer in isolation then receive the light and thrive like a flower bathing in the sun.

It takes courage to leave the old neighborhood of habits. Life feels safer there. But it sure ain't easier. We forfeit help, comradery, and a quicker way to the goal. The following incident when I lived in Greece illustrates this:

Life placed one of its helpers right in front of me. She was in a plain, dark blue suit of no distinct markings or logo. I couldn't tell whether she was a regular store employee, a product representative, or something of both. She said nothing. Not a "Can I help you?" nor a sales pitch. Plenty of shoppers were going by. She stood close to an island of detergents and glanced here and there, at one person then another, shifting from one foot the other. She was inconspicuous, yet begging for attention at the same time.

Why the discomfort? What was eating away her insides? It seemed much more than the normal antsiness to finish work and dash out the door.

I felt for this girl. Secretly I hoped that someone would go up to her and pull her out of herself, at least divert her attention from her self-torment. I walked by her three times searching for groceries. On each pass, I stepped resolutely around her and purposely averted my eyes.

To be honest, her presence triggered my own uneasiness. I was embarrassed because I couldn't find any light bulbs. (Shopping at the local supermarket in a foreign-speaking country can do it.) Of course, the supermarket had them, I wasn't in Antarctica. I searched both floors. Nothing. Now I'd have to ask. I knew the word in Greek. I could always mime it, too.

The girl probably would have lit up like one of those light bulbs if I had asked with my accent. I didn't. I left the supermarket empty handed, perplexed, and with my stupid do-it-yourself pride intact.

The light bulbs were right down the aisle where she stood.

My wife later asked me, "Did you ask anyone?" A pathetic "No" driveled out of my mouth.

The line from the play *Auntie Mame* sums it up well: "Life is a banquet, and most poor suckers are starving to death." I was the sucker. I didn't reach out. The setup was perfect. The girl was there, ready to serve. She was the main part of the feast. Her discomfort was like a big flag waving to me, saying, "Hey, over here, and let me show you, and we'll both feel better." It was irrelevant whether she knew where the light bulbs were or not.

DIVINE DEEPENING

How do feel when you help someone who asks?
It's your turn: Ask, and watch the feast begin.

Can there be unity
without offering ourselves?

SELF-JUSTIFIED AND NOWHERE TO GO

Holding too tightly to your position can lead to a stubborn standoff. You know you're right; your partner thinks they're right. You argue. Neither of you wants to give in. Listening is at twenty percent, maybe; reacting is a defiant eighty percent or more. Reason has abdicated. Emotion rules like a rifle. You and your partner retreat into your individual hurts.

Separation is plain ugly and painful. All because of stupid egos butting up against each other needing to prove and preserve. Separation can then breed more heavily armored bodies and hardened minds bent on protecting wrongly positioned hearts. Whereas in truth minds need to step aside and allow hearts back in the game.

The whole key for me is sensing when I am losing someone. When they are beginning to turn off and close down. If I am aware (and courageous enough to summon up humility), right then I can step back, take off the gloves, swallow my bullheadedness, and listen—even offer an *I'm sorry*, if I am that big.

Here is one of my wake-up calls and how it affected a work relationship. I was at the home of a friend's parents in Brooklyn, New York. We had taken the subway from Manhattan. We walked in the door and barely had been seated when the couple started kibitzing over something so mundane that I had forgotten it by the time the evening ended. They stood hunched over their chairs at opposite ends of the table facing each other like aged gunslingers. Neither budged and kept firing their crotchety retorts at each other as my friend unsuccessfully attempted to back them off each other. (I sensed that he'd witnessed this showdown plenty of times.)

For most hosts, I imagined this would have been embarrassing: a couple married uncountable years going at it with abandon in front of a guest. For them, their son's friend simply had to wait. Hey, they were being honest. Though the scene had a sobering effect on me. I realized that each of them probably had been hanging onto their sacrosanct opinions since day one of the relationship and were not about to give in at this late stage. Anyone in range would just have to weather their uncomfortable comfort zone until one or the other gave in, or passed away.

Would I end up in the same rut, I wondered, as I fought with my dearest one simply because I refused to let go of some treasured view? I hoped not.

The evening ended, giving me plenty to reflect upon.

My resolve was put to the test shortly after at PEOPLE Magazine, of all places.

It was a Monday afternoon, the first closing day of the magazine. On Mondays, proofreaders had plenty of downtime waiting for edited copy. My partner for the shift was Rick. Rick was a friendly, talkative guy with one unusual characteristic: He was an avowed Marxist-Leninist who proudly wore a long, heavy forest green coat of Russian Army vintage. He was planning on attending an upcoming Leninist convention in Moscow as he had done in the past.

We got into a discussion about CIA activities in Central America. This was way out of my league, but I couldn't let him have his way. Rick's anti-American slant on the whole thing got me going. His argument first took us into one country overthrowing their government, then it advanced into another country a few years later sabotaging their regime. I offered some lame, uninformed defenses of U.S. activity, which Rick jumped all over with counterclaims. He seemed so down on the U.S. that after one of his points I bluntly stated that living in Russia was always an option. Rick was nonplussed. He casually remarked he had thought about the very idea.

Not long into our discussion it dawned on me: one, it was futile to argue any of these points since I had little knowledge of foreign policy and two, the clandestine U.S. aggression that we were debating now had become a minor skirmish between us.

A skirmish that clearly wasn't worthwhile: I was losing Rick, basically a very nice guy who I sit next to, and my peace. I abruptly dropped our conversation. Rick accepted and we went back to our reading as friends.

How often, I thought, do I completely miss the point. Yeah, my pride is preserved. I didn't back down; won a few exchanges; showed I could deal. I might even have had the last say.

But have I gained? Has the exchange made us closer? Is my heart more open? If the answer is negative for either, then it's time to retreat for a little self-reflection or be crowned alone in my glorious opinions and think I've come somewhere.

DIVINE DEEPENING

If you distance the very ones
you want to win over, then what's
your next move?

National identities, racial identities,
religious identities, family identities,
sexual identities, job identities,
school identities, species identities—
Strip these away and what's left:
Love, kindness, respect—
A unifying identity.
Let's stick to that.

HANDHOLDING ON HIGH

As a young boy, it seemed right and natural to be friendly with everyone. Why stick to only the smart kids if I got good grades? The athletes of the class if I was athletic? The "cool ones" if I was considered cool?

Those identities felt limiting even to my grade school mind, although many kids seemed to play up to them. It was understandable. Who wouldn't want to be accepted? Life doesn't get any better than that. Being one of the smarter ones, who also was tenacious in schoolyard sports, and not socially awkward meant I was pretty much "in."

As I got into middle school, I began to see a shifting of alliances among friends. Friends would go in and out of favor and back in again. I didn't get it. I was nice to everyone. I was bothered to see how mean-spirited my friends could be. One friend who had long hair and played guitar got tossed into a dumpster of garbage by my jock friends. I recall his embarrassed attempt at a smile as he emerged: He still wanted to fit in despite the mistreatment. I felt bad for what they did to him but I let my "in" status override my desire to speak up about how unfairly they were treating him.

Mocking others seemed cruel and unfounded. If someone was different, they were different. Was I any better because I had lots of friends? Had I made it somewhere? I was friendly with classmates whether we hung or not. I still am. I want to be comfortable hanging with anyone, irrespective of rank, race, religion, etc., and I want them to be confortable hanging with me. Can't do that if I'm plastering labels over those who don't fit into my worldview.

All of us are in the process of overcoming limiting backgrounds. That is, conceptions of ourselves which confine us to certain peoples, places, jobs, and lifestyles. I was raised in one neighborhood, in a small town, in basically one socio-economic ethnic group, and attended parochial schools through high school. I was exposed to little more than any of my friends. I credit my parents' open-mindedness for helping to bring out in me tolerance and respect for friends and strangers unlike me.

Unity in diversity became my passion.

Being an athlete my quest was best epitomized by the Olympic Games. I wanted to compete in them, especially track and field. I never made it. Though I funded my way to the Games twice. The Olympics, with their interlaced five-colored rings of the different continents, symbolize man's unity in common pursuit of excellence. I witnessed peoples of every make and model come together and harmoniously play and compete. They didn't need to know the others' languages, customs, religion, or political beliefs. They only needed a level playing field, and friendship reigned.

I am still touched to see the handshakes, shoulder pats and hugs of rivals who have just completed the biggest event of their lives on one of the world's greatest stages. Decathletes, especially, epitomize comradery. They are out there two long, grueling days. Each is aware of the effort, skills and dedication necessary to be there and master 10 very different events. They are competing, no doubt. And their mutual respect and shared purpose lifts them together to the heights of athleticism.

I never cared for popularity. It comes and goes, as I saw in middle school. Connecting with someone's heart has been the most important thing in any relationship. If I am genuinely interested the other person feels it. It is an invitation for them to be themselves and come closer. If I hold myself separate for whatever reason, they know it.

College graduation bore this out for me. Elections were coming up for a two-year appointment to the college's board of trustees. I decided to apply. I had served the college as a dorm resident advisor, sat on a college administration committee and organized a campus-wide running event for Thanksgiving. Running for the board was another opportunity to represent my fellow students. The two other candidates were the student body president and the senior class president. They had the public leadership thing going for them. But I sensed I would win because of the wider range of students I related with as opposed to the more stratified circles they ran with. I did win.

One of the blessings of the two-year position was a new level of people to relate to. I served on the board with a man who had masterminded an escape from a German concentration camp in World War II and who was a friend of the then current U.S. President. He was a model of principle and of heart fused into one. His warm, direct manner of engaging fellow board members' concerns drew each of us to him like a magnet. Especially he taught me that when you listen with genuine interest others feel it and more freely share of themselves.

A few years out of college I headed to New York to do theater. Without realizing it, acting was the perfect next step in enlarging my empathy with those from very different walks of life. I would walk the streets, carefully observe someone who caught my fancy, and then recreate them in the acting studio for others.

The acting process was either outside-in (put on the clothes, the mannerisms, walk, and voice inflections, a la Olivier, and see what feelings arise); or inside-out (use empathy and personal memories brought up that felt akin to the character I was recreating to best exemplify their external behavior). Either way I was overcoming my sense of separation, along with judgments, to become like someone else. Perhaps the real gift was allowing others a way of getting closer to the life of a person they would never meet nor want to meet.

In one of my acting forays, I found myself standing next to a homeless man on a cold winter day as he warmed his hands over a fire in a barrel between Avenues B and C, a drug-infested area of the Lower East Side. Simple wisdom poured out of him. I listened. No longer was it about acting, observing, or any of that. One man was sharing his story. Another was held in the grace of it.

Lately, I've been engaged in outreach work in the heart of the city I live in. Opportunities abound to meet strangers, make friends, and lend a kind word or two to those from a wide cross section of the city. I get to take part in the treasury of their lives. By letting go of the picture in front of me, be it a smelly, unkempt homeless man who seems to need and need, or the perfectly groomed self-satisfied exec who resolutely strides past, I position myself at the door of their hearts. When that special moment arrives for us to touch, they are a bit freer and easier to be who they are, to express their struggles, their beauty, their hopes, or their simple curiosity of who I am.

This is handholding on high, the kind I envisioned as a boy.

DIVINE DEEPENING

Is your heart readily accessible, or in check
by jaded conceptions of how another
must appear to you?

MEDITATION

The Universal Glue

Love attracts. Love unites. Love is the force that holds absolutely everything together. You, me, relationships of every ilk, governments, the air we breathe, the earth, sun, galaxies, black and white holes, right on down to the tiniest, most insignificant particles in the universe—all are wedded by love. When love seemingly isn't present, people move apart. But that's mainly because they have forgotten love is still there.

You are the center of love. You are a universe of love. Love is your life. Wherever you are is the sacred abode of love. As well, every person and place outside of you is the abode of love. Imagine that you are wrapped in a womb of loving tenderness. What does that feel like? Allow all tension to be gently consumed out of you by the womb of love you are in. Imagine a perfectly secure sense of well-being engulfing you—and it is permanent. Feel a softness permeate you like never before.

When ready, switch gears and bring up anything that you've held onto—bad attitudes, self-judgments, criticisms, character faults— and expose them to love. Let them unravel in the atmosphere of love. Whatever comes into thought, give it up. Offer it to the force field of love you are in and are generating. When it seems like there is nothing more, ask, wait, and see if anything else appears needing to be led into love. Sense how connected you are getting to yourself. That's self-love.

While dwelling in this fount of your purity and love invite all your loved ones and best friends in. See the warmth glue you together. Feel the closeness grow. Now choose one of them or someone outside your circle you haven't felt as close to or even animosity toward. Bring them into your sacred place. Remember, let love lead, not personal will. Love fills the space between you two. Watch love dissolve the jagged edges and the old hurts until all that's left is the flow of goodwill embracing you both. Thank them and everyone else who came and dwelled with you.

Take a deep breath and integrate any feelings that have come up into your body. Remember to dwell continuously in the abode of love. It is always right there comforting you and connecting you to all life.

6
CHAPTER

REVELATIONS: INSTANT AND OTHERWISE

My own opinions interest me less than
listening for the heart of the matter.

THE HANDS OF THE DIRECTOR

He seemed odd and emotionally distant, as if he were locked away in a busy corner of himself. I half-expected him to bump into the walls of the school as he walked through. I'd brush by him and could see monologues playing and replaying in his head, which I suppose is normal for an acting teacher.

In acting school, you are taught to *be there*, above everything else. This means relating to the environment and the person next to you. The head acting teacher, who also was director of the theater school, was very present when he demonstrated technique or taught. He had a sharp eye, was boyishly enthusiastic and often flew out of his chair onto the stage to give a pointer and to show some aspect of stagecraft. Once when I was acting in front of class he stopped me, stepped out next to me, and had me count the floorboards. I felt my aura shrink into me as I imagined how I must have appeared *not to be there*.

When not onstage teaching and demonstrating, the director just looked off. I imagined that his over-sized, slightly lopsided head had something to do with it. He was up there, filling some part of it. The diction he retained from his training in the English theater system reinforced the discomforting space he held between himself and others. Fronting that affectation were his big teeth. They would mash together creating wads of saliva that continually threatened to spill out of his mouth and sully his proper way of speaking.

He looked a mess. His shirt was never quite tucked in. His suit often hung to one side or the other. He'd arrive to class looking as if he'd slept in his clothes, or on them. As for his hair, forget it. It had taken too many turns trying to follow his internal monologues and now was draped the way it wanted to be.

He would have made a great character study. We actors were running around Manhattan observing bums, prostitutes, street vendors, you name it, but we didn't realize the gold mine of humanity right in front of us. I sure didn't, until we spoke one day. To me, he was strange, like one of those theater students I would meet in New York who seem out of touch with the reality they were trying to portray.

The day came for my conference with him. I was very interested in what he would say. We started with slow chitchat, then he switched tracks. He leaned forward in a slow, deliberate manner and cupped his hands together as if he was holding a special gift and said, "Our parents give us their bag of talents, difficulties, gifts, and phobias," i.e., their endowment. (His hands remained cupped together in the air, halfway toward me.) "We take the bag and either open it up, take a good look and work with what's there, thereby changing it and ourselves in the process, or we don't deal with what's in the bag and simply pass it along, unopened, to *our* children."

Whoa, his cupped hands really had held a gem, of sorts. I had a newfound respect for him. We didn't go much further into it since he saw that I had gotten his point—my emotions were jammed up, which was affecting my acting, and I had the choice to look at myself.

That summer the bag spilled open right in my face. I saw things I didn't want to. I struggled with things I thought I should have been done with. A whirlwind of emotions stirred. The work had begun, and the work will continue as long as I am willing to keep opening the bag and straightening out the business needing my attention.

I liken the process to a baseball diamond. I'm on first base and a hit advances me to third. Life says, "Great, you've learned how to go directly from first to third. Now go back to first and learn how to run intelligently to second—taking big leads, stealing the base, hopping over hit balls, sliding into the bag feet first, then hands first." I go crazy. I just want to be on second.

Eventually I'll master that base path. Then, Life will invite me to master the path from second to third and third to home. When I've completed the base running and am safely home, there'll be no more need of the baseball diamond. Life will respond, "Well done, have a breather and exult a bit. Then, head over to the other ballpark. It's a much bigger game."

DIVINE DEEPENING

Choose someone in your life whom you are
not enamored with.
What gift does their presence offer you?
What attitude in you will allow you to
receive their gift?

If you fill your own shoes,
then you are never out of step.

TOILET TRAINING

Is there enlightenment in a toilet bowl? Yup, can be. It depends on how committed I am willing to be. Any insight I can divine that lifts me higher I go with. Where I am at the moment is what I have to work with. If I accept myself being there, I have a chance at reaping the present, whether I like my lot or not.

As I headed toward the men's room, one thing was clear: I wasn't having visions of paradise, I was going to clean toilets . . . and not expecting a thing. I was doing my job. One of my tasks for the day was getting the bathrooms ready for the evening's Jewish Seder. Being the sexton at a Unitarian-Universalist church meant doing almost anything from setting up and breaking down chairs and tables for all kinds of events to weekly rounds of scrubbing, vacuuming, sweeping, to climbing way up to the bell tower every Friday and winding the town clock while yellow jackets swarmed overhead.

I put on my orange rubber gloves, selected my workmates (a bucket, toilet bowl brush and new toilet cleaner) and headed for a toilet. A few resistant thoughts greeted me as I walked in, *I've been here before. Whoop-de-do.* Then, my thought rallied, *Enough, I have work to do.*

I read the directions: Lift the seat cover. Open the spout. Squirt the blue liquid under the rim, down the sides and into the heart of the bowl. Grab a toilet bowl brush and begin to scrub. Okay. Somehow, reading the directions locked me in almost super-sensibly to being right there in the bowl cleaning: under the rim; down the sides into the porcelain depths; up and around; scrubbing the bowl for whiteness, and for them, the parishioners and guests.

The thought, *for them,* sunk in. I was cleaning for them. Purifying the toilet bowl. They could come into purity and release themselves—they were infinitely worth it. I wept with joy, gratitude, and appreciation for the work at hand as I finished swooshing through the blue waters.

As I straightened up to leave the thought came, *Was I being foolish? Getting a spiritual lift over . . . No,* a voice said, *don't censure yourself.* I happily exited. Next step, the ladies' room.

DIVINE DEEPENING

Become very present, almost super-attentive,
in the job at hand
and see if your commitment frees you from
being a slave to it.

Disgruntled waiting is life lost.
Patient alertness is Being fulfilled.

A REVELATION OF DELAYS

I woke up calm and optimistic. Another beautiful day in Greece. I meditated. I did my exercises. I checked my schedule. I was ready to leap into my day. What I leapt into was a big, resounding, *Not today!*

My first errand was at the town hall of a nearby suburb. I went there to pay for my ad in the monthly paper. The man steadfastly refused to take the money, saying that it was too early. I tried convincing him with a sense of urgency. No way. A Greek male in charge is not apt to budge unless you overpower him with higher connections (authority) than his. I walked out a bit mystified. Who wouldn't want to take an early payment? Well, I could hold onto a few extra drachmas for a time.

I then hiked over to the local post office to mail announcements for my fall program. The clerk said, "We can't mail them without a proper envelope, or you can try but we don't normally accept them and I can't guarantee that they'll be delivered." I felt discouraged. Now I needed to rewrite all the addresses. Well, at least the announcements wouldn't get lost in the shuffle.

I left and headed to the stationery store where I had ordered a stamp with my name and address on it. The clerk said, "I'm sorry. I forgot to tell them to bring it. Try tomorrow about the same hour." This was the second time the stamp had been delayed. I walked out angry.

Rules, regulations, forgetfulness—doors were slamming in my face and on my day. On the walk to my motorbike, I began to get it: The rhythm for the day was not a smooth checklist. There was no one to curse, and I knew it. Life was moving at a pace I didn't expect.

How foolish to take it personally, I thought, and get into a thing with everyone in my path. Equally dumb would be to chalk it up to a Greek mentality— as if Greeks universally postpone what they could do today (although I was tempted, knowing how long I often had to wait for basic services in Athens). I would rather catch the pattern right at the start of my day. I have found myself in reoccurring daily patterns and done my best to get wind of them before they dragged a frustrated Mark all over creation.

Who wants to run head-on into car after car and finally realize you've been going down one-way streets the wrong way all day. I prefer to grab hold of myself with a *Hey you, wake up. A car* (a stubborn pattern) *is coming straight at you*. Then, I can reverse gears and get into a better track fast.

What about being awake and alert from the start by asking, What does the Divine want me to do? Call first? Trust and charge out the door? Stay put and allow the day to unfold? I chose to charge out and trust— my habituated action mode. Discovering I needed to change envelope sizes necessitated writing addresses again. But the delay enabled me to use the new ink stamp address on each envelope, which I wanted to do in the first place. The envelopes looked more professional. And one week after the man refused to take the ad money, I received an offer to place an ad in a newspaper that specifically targeted the audience I wanted to reach. So, I cancelled the first ad, used the money for the better ad, and saved more running around in the process. Those delays were worth it.

DIVINE DEEPENING

Be a merciless warrior with yourself and respond to this:
In what area of your life are you obstinately sticking to a course of action that is no longer serving you? Are you willing to make the necessary changes?

*Force a flower open
and the beauty withers in your hand
The meek shall inherit the earth. **

*(Psalm 37:11)

ON BEING RIPE

Tony, our landlord, finished fiddling with the bulkhead lock and straightened up into my hellos. I was a tad wary of engaging Tony. He could take a tidbit and talk it up a tree and around the block without the least concern that you went on the journey with him. Tony was as friendly and impassioned as you'd find in an Italian neighbor. He just never stopped talking—and I usually had extracted the juice a few sentences into his monologue.

On this particular day, I resolved to go the distance with him. I wouldn't jerk myself away from his good-will as if I had something to do. We stood by the grape arbor. Tony's discourse on grape picking was fine with me. Grapes are a love of mine. Particularly the deep bluish Concord variety hanging right over our heads.

"My father used to let them (the grapes) go till right before Columbus Day. The bees would swarm all over the grapes trying to get at their sweetness. They were like honey in your mouth," Tony exclaimed, as his nose and mouth became one, sensuous grape rapture. Unbeknownst to Tony, my jaw had dropped open. *As late as Columbus Day* reverberated through me. I was stunned, and instantaneously illuminated. I blessed Tony (inwardly), thanking him for his father's wisdom.

Years of ignorant, impatient picking had been erased in a few sentences. The key was simply to wait. Those many late, late summer afternoons I had crouched under the grapevines on the rusted tin roof of Mr. McNichol's empty chicken and rabbit coop munching on Concord grapes came back. Twenty minutes, a half hour, I could never tell how long I had been there. It was supreme happiness: laying on the warm tin, swimming in green leaves and vines with cluster after cluster of dangling, purplish-blue prizes peeking out from the green or set right in front of my eyes, and the self-satisfying act of my hand moving out at just the right angle to pluck one.

I'd slide out of my grape tangle, step on and then bounce off the sagging wire fence into the back corner of our garden with a happy feeling in my gut. How I ate supper after my grape fests, I'll never know.

The bliss remains in my mind. Yet the acidic-n-sweet mix that ended in my stomach now rings sour. The grapes weren't quite ready and were telling me: Their color wasn't yet the chalky, deep, bluish-black of October; their skin was a tad too taught; and their aroma hadn't matured to a sweet, earthy musk that drenches the air and swells your nose and makes you stop like a drunken yellow jacket and stick your face into the nearest juicy one.

Picking as I had done for so long not only insulted my belly, it was like an unsavory habit that perpetuates the same ol' result. My actions weren't the gentle twist off or peeling away of the grape from its gel-like stem, but more of a willed, staccato tug somewhat analogous to kissing a girl who isn't into kissing you—a semi-sweet victory that quickly reveals a hollow, dry aftertaste.

Here it is the end of the first week of October. I have checked the grapes daily since my talk with Tony. I am the watchful father. Removing the rotten, noting the darkening, feeling for softness, tugging gently for willingness, and sampling a grape here, a grape there.

The time has come. Patience has yielded her gift: healthy, plump-n-juicy, infinitely sweeter grapes than I can remember. I am blessed to realize ripeness.

DIVINE DEEPENING
Are you impatient with a recurring situation?
What might life be trying to tell you?
Tune into your body when impatience
grabs you and ask.

Does my life declare my truth?
Is my life layered in untruths?
Here's one litmus test:
Am I being myself no matter what
the circumstances?

THE PRICE OF PAINT REMOVAL

A good friend of mine living on the Upper West Side of Manhattan was going on tour with the Joffrey Ballet and asked me to watch her apartment. She casually mentioned that at some point she wanted to strip the wooden mantelpiece that fronted the fireplace. I decided to surprise her.

I arrived the day after she hit the road with tools in hand. I learned quickly that the paint would not come off without a serious commitment. Too bad, I wanted this to be a few evenings of a whack and a stroke and it's off. There were layers of white paint and a concealed one of putrid green to tackle. In spots, they seemed bonded for life. In a sense, they would have been, if I hadn't come along. Wads of plaster were glommed into the wood and paint. How best to attack without destroying the wood? Every day was a struggle to find the right technique, the better angle to apply force, but not too much. I'd go over small areas, first chipping, then scraping, next applying paint remover if I was close to the wood, and going somewhere else and repeating the process. Then returning to the original spot, scraping what had flaked up, often not being satisfied, and intensify my concentration as I bore down toward the bare beauty. Finding a working rhythm seemed as difficult as exposing the wood.

When a clean patch of wood appeared it was like beholding a patch of truth that had been sleeping beneath the caked rubble of years and now was revealing its real nature.

I worked my fingers hard. Some days I toiled in the mornings and evenings. The work was both tedious, doing basically the same stroke for hours, and exciting: I wasn't sure exactly what I would find under the thick blobs of paint and plaster.

One day while chipping away, I discovered a tightly spaced row of teeth jutting down the entire length of the mantel piece. Each was about an inch across and nearly three inches high. I was thrilled, and, given their size, amazed how they could have remained hidden. My elation lasted about a minute: I knew the sheer number of teeth and their tight bunching would require three times the labor to finely scrape and sand each of them into an acceptable condition.

That's how it goes: honest work leading to more work. In short, I was uncovering the extent of my effort as much as the wood in waiting. Occasional mistakes occurred as I attempted to muscle off years of coating in one blow. To see even small flakes of wood fly off was painful. The artistry was emerging and I didn't want to lose a speck of it.

Working across the front—above the teeth and below the mantle lip—I made my biggest find: a delicate, interwoven leaf pattern. Who would cover up such beauty? More finesse was now called for. I applied slower, more measured applications of tool and force. I didn't want to mar a single tendril of the dance of leaves emerging.

Finally, all the paint was off. I sanded with progressively finer grades of sandpaper. I measured my strokes to be sure every edge of teeth and leaves was smooth and well-defined. Next, I rubbed in linseed oil. I began with a cloth, but usually ended up using my fingers. The direct contact of fingers, oil, and wood felt more thorough and caring.

The wood was alive again. A natural sheen and lovely lines showered the room with elegance. Covering over the original craftsmanship now seemed incomprehensible and almost criminal.

I have realized that stripping the wooden mantelpiece years ago was a metaphor for my life. The calloused facades I held to, of accumulated heaviness on my soul, patterns of hardness, pride, edginess, and unwillingness to yield self, had to be exposed, confronted, softened, cried through, and washed clean with self-love, forgiveness, and better ideas of who I really am so that my heart could finally breathe and my true colors show forth.

DIVINE DEEPENING

What attitude tweaks are needed
to let your facades go?

Of old, hands folded in a pleading
Save us, Lord.
Today, hands unfolded receiving
what's divinely ours.

TURNING THE SHROUD AROUND

My Rudra meditation group from New York had finished our retreat on the Italian Riviera outside of Genoa. My girlfriend and I decided to train the two plus hours to Torino (Turin) to see the Shroud of Turin. Once there we headed straight to the cathedral where it was kept.

I now sat against a stone pillar of the church entrance. The church attendant had just closed the doors on us. I felt like an outcast. Inside, locked away was the prize—a priceless image of history's greatest figure. I was so close. But, it was no-go. No peeks. Not even a proper sniff. I could have been on the other side of the planet. Why be here?

The lousy five minutes inside the Turin cathedral had been enough to skim over the history of the Shroud, get a few Shroud cards, and be turned out. What did I expect anyway, a cardinal from Rome arrayed in his finest vestments to emerge from the vestibule and drape the Shroud over my arm? Come on, Mark. (According to Wikipedia, the Shroud has been on public display only 19 times since its history began).

Still, I refused to accept that I had come all the way by train for this. There had to be something here for me.

The question got me moving out of my moping and into the real practice of asking and demanding to know.

I wasn't quite there, though. My disappointment with organized religion had been rekindled. My mind was left ruminating over an image in a rare parade, which is not something that fed my soul. I wanted more—a real taste of something that I felt was straight out of the guiding hand of Spirit, here and now.

I had to quiet my thoughts. I told my girlfriend that I needed to be alone for a few and she graciously stepped away. I knew something was here for me. But what?

Just like an air-filled ball held underwater and released, the answer popped into view: The solution was not in the Shroud, but in my heart. Of course, right inside was the real prize I sought.

I felt relieved, even elated. This is what Turin had for me. The Shroud faded from thought. I grabbed my girlfriend and we rushed off to eat at a small bistro on a side street off the piazza. We ordered. I slowly told her about the realization I had in front of the church.

While speaking, a shaft of illumination engulfed me. My soul was drawn upwards and held in an exalted state of joy that we all crave but seldom get to taste. There were no words or thoughts, just a consuming light, showing me the way, giving me the go-ahead to step into my spiritual destiny, to be a vehicle of Spirit. Tears came like a rich appetizer.

DIVINE DEEPENING

Your desire doesn't manifest. Do you react
with frustration? Unhappiness? Self-torture?
Can you ask, listen, and trust God
to reveal your next steps?

When we cease in our longings,
what's left?
More space to receive

FROM GOD

When I earnestly began my spiritual practice years ago, a question kept coming in meditations: How do I know if a thought is from God or self-will? It seemed nearly impossible to discern what was what. God seemed hidden somewhere behind an opaque screen. He was not a present and near help I could lean on in bad times. My up and down thoughts about myself further muddied the God and self-will dilemma. One day I'd bounce down New York City streets feeling joyful and on my game. The next day I'd feel chaffed and on edge and justify my mess with some earth-battered story about myself. I felt like a pendulum swinging between heaven and hell.

I erroneously accepted the ride, which perpetuated the tortured model of myself I had grown up with: me angel, me devil.

My mother had wrestled with the concept of the human and the Divine, too. How could a sweet little baby come into the world tainted, she wondered, when they are so pure? What did they do wrong? It didn't make sense to her. As a hospital delivery room nurse, she daily witnessed the love newborns inspire in us. She was deeply disturbed that they were somehow "sentenced" by her church's moral dictums from the get-go, as was I with its unavoidable outcome: I was a sinful mortal who must regularly be absolved of evil tendencies. The idea of being at the bottom of a spiritual hierarchy felt disheartening. God felt out of reach.

By the time I finished my parochial school education I decided that if God had created us this way—as beings far from heaven—I wasn't interested. This was not a God I could respect or have any desire to turn to. I severed my religious ties. I would go it alone and find the Divine another way.

The search for Truth (or what at the time I termed "limitlessness") took me in many directions. One period it was love of the absolute nature of mathematics; next, singing the highest, purest note; then pushing past limits in marathon running. My Truth quest eventually landed me at the feet of love. Love was the biggie. Discovering its possibilities was the ultimate, and would take me on a spiritual adventure all over the globe.

I got into deeper relationships; began studying meditation; trained as a shiatsu therapist; worked with spiritual healers from New York to Alaska to Greece; and made pilgrimages to the Four Corners on Navajo land, Italy, Israel, India, and a Tibetan monastery in the Himalayas. I was probably like the baby bird in the P. D. Eastman book who goes to and fro asking the question, "Are you my mother?"

Like the eastern sadhu who says, "not this," "not this," to world delusions posing as their reality, I, too, couldn't settle for a partial salvation, one that didn't ring true to the core. I would give all of myself, and wear the clothes (the beliefs and rituals) as if they were truly me. Then, the old, unsettled yearning for Truth would impel me on.

I eventually landed in Greece, teaching meditation and shiatsu. I healed a few people instantaneously. I understood these healings to be God hearing my cries and freeing a disturbed mind. The focus on me as the healer, with my 'blessed hands', was cool and flattering but didn't feel altogether right. I knew the spiritual force that did the healing was greater than me. Why, I wondered, couldn't anyone learn to do the healings? Also, how could the healing work be consistent, and repeated, rather than an out-of-the-blue miracle?

Those questions led to a shift away from manipulation of the body to a desire to rely solely on Spirit.

I returned to the States with my new family—my Greek wife, her son, and my one-year-old daughter. While living in Boston a friend gave us the book *Science and Health with Key to the Scriptures* by Mary Baker Eddy, a woman who had healed the sick instantaneously in the mid-1800s. I was impressed how the book claimed I could know God. Was that possible? The idea of God seemed too vast to ever wrap my head

around. I was skeptical, but kept reading. The absolute nature of many statements came across like pile
drivers, hammering concepts down with a relentless
certainty. I was stirred up and almost couldn't bear
it—how could anyone make such definitive claims?
I had studied books on spirituality. They talked spiritual. Gave glimpses of God. Even lifted me. This book
came straight into thought and immediately began
revamping my sense of life.

One statement in particular changed everything:
"Jesus beheld in Science the perfect man, who appeared
to him where sinning mortal man appears to mortals.
In this perfect man, the Savior saw God's own likeness,
and this correct view of man healed the sick. Thus,
Jesus taught that the kingdom of God is intact, universal, and that man is pure and holy."* The veil over
my eyes that had separated me from God was ripped
off by those words. The supposed dark side of my soul
was exposed for what is, the wrong way of looking at
myself and a myth that God, good, had ever created a
man opposite in nature from Its own purity, goodness,
and love.

The slate was wiped clean—I was innocent like a
newborn. An unimaginable lightness swept through
me, and I wept. Moreover, my Father-Mother God was
finally near, dear, natural, logical, and inevitable.

While sitting and meditating beside the dining room table on a day off recently, a thought about being an accident-prone sufferer came up, and it was met by a voice that boomed out of me, "Not from God," then a thought tempting me to react about a trying relationship, "Not from God ," then a thought of harmony and love in my family, "From God." Each thought— and they were coming like rushing waves—called up a loud and decisive, "From God," or "Not from God." The affirmation and denial process touched upon nearly every major aspect of my life.

I now could take a stand and know without a doubt whether a thought was from God or from a mind that separates me from myself and others through confusion, discord, fear, and judgment.

*Mary Baker Eddy, *Science and Health with Key to the Scriptures* (Boston: The Christian Science Board of Directors 1971), 476.

DIVINE DEEPENING
Spiritual concerns aside, how do you know
whether to heed the voice you hear or not?
What is your criteria?

MEDITATION

Listening for Wisdom

Get comfortable. Let go of the day with a few conscious breaths. Release those must-do's as you go into the Silence. Give yourself completely to this one act of being here. Imagine that your life is dependent on you tuning into the stillness of your being. You have never done anything more important.

Extraneous thoughts or emotions may try you. Don't question or fight them—allow them their say and let them be.

Focus your attention on the light within, in particular the consciousness that you are a ray of enlightened awareness connected to the Divine. Tune into this idea of being a ray of intelligence emanating from an infinitely wise Source. See yourself merging with this brilliance. Know it is lasting. Know it is always there for you. It is your bliss, your bastion of wisdom within. Trust that any answers you need are waiting there in the light.

Now bring up (without coloring attitudes) anything in you that needs an answer. Offer it, or place it, into the light of your bliss. Let it marinate there. Whatever it is, it cannot trouble you since it is surrounded by enlightenment. The issue is being well taken care of and can only dissolve in the light. Listen for any message that this situation might need to convey to you. If something comes, awesome, be grateful for the gift. If not, that's fine. The light will reveal anything you need to know.

Be aware of any feelings and thoughts as you end the meditation. Offer them, too, to the wisdom of the light within. Feel free to write down inspiration and revelations that came to you. Know that you can access infinite wisdom any time and any place. It is yours.

7
CHAPTER

GRACE

Am I serene as an evergreen
whose arms yield as gracefully
to the snow piling up as to its melting?

A GRACE SO SOON

Isn't it natural to want to savor the moments that fill you with the most happiness? To let joy percolate through your being and just stay there—especially when it's the birth of your first child.

When I first held my daughter, I thought my heart would burst. Never had I felt such love and tenderness. All my spiritual training and tear-filled raptures about divine Oneness were reset. I was literally face to face with the heart of my spiritual journey. I was now part of a universal tribe of men who discover love in their firstborn.

You would think that with my babe in my arms nothing could touch or interfere with the joyful flood of emotions—they are here to stay. Indeed, they have. But there was a bittersweet aspect of her birth. And maybe this is the lesson that all mothers must go through the moment those nine months are up.

The attending doctor was supportive of my wife's and my desire to have a natural birth. Once in the hospital, it became clear the labor was not moving along easily in that direction. The screams next door were not helping either. The doctor came in a few times, checked Maria and informed us of us her lack of progress. I could see she was struggling. We used whatever we understood to keep her relaxed and optimistic. After a long while we relented and opted to get our baby out the fast way.

My wife was on the table shivering under the lights. I sat on a stool in the far corner of the operating room watching. (The doctor had graciously allowed me to witness the C-section.) As the doctor deepened his incisions I began to feel wheezy, as if I would pass out. I breathed deeply, centered myself, breathed more, and remained as conscious as I could of the cool, sterile environment. I was composed when the doctor reached in and pulled out our steamy, wet baby. The cord was cut; he handed the baby to a nurse; she handed off to another nurse who brought our baby to a station and held her upside down to drain the water and mucus from her lungs. As I watched from the stool, from what felt like an unfordable gulf of space from her, it came to me:

She (my daughter) *is for the world. Look how three pairs of hands, three people I don't really know, and she doesn't know, have handled her before me. She isn't really mine. Yes, I'm principal caretaker for a while. But I must let her go right now, right from the start.*

I cried as I sat there watching others handle my baby. I didn't want this realization so soon. I knew it was a gift, but couldn't I have had a grace period. I reluctantly accepted knowing somewhere in me that grace has no periods; it comes when it comes. My job is to recognize it and receive it.

A minute later we were off to give her a proper washing. Then the glorious moment of holding her the first time and showing her off to my in-laws standing behind the glass window. Now the lovefest could begin.

Those early hours of her birth in Greece are long gone. The interim has been a beautiful father-daughter adventure. She now is a few thousand miles away going to college in California and I've had to reacquaint myself with letting her go once again and trusting. No freebie for my heart. With texting and Facebook our journey apart isn't half so hard. Besides, I know Love's caring hands are handing her off every step of the way as they did that night in the Athens hospital when she arrived.

DIVINE DEEPENING

What human attachment are you unwilling to
let go of
that is depriving you and the other person of
fully living?
Will you live in this question?

Watch a newborn sleep through
a hailstorm of adult yapping.
What peace, what focus,
What transcendence it offers us.

THIS IS HOW WE FIT

for Maria and Natalia

There, mother and child lay
Under the downy comforter
With sleeping heads
Drawn
Lovingly together (a temple on a cheek)
In the billow of pillows

A sweet n' steady pulse
Of deep breaths stream out
Of their wintry warm dreams
Rolling over each other
Enveloping me in
        A visage of heaven
        Resting below
        My gaze

This is how we fit—
No distance, no "mine"
Just a distilling of dawn
And of two into one
Pure, peaceful embrace.

DIVINE DEEPENING

Feeling disconnected?
Curl up with your love, your baby, your pet
and feel the warmth spread in you.

GRACE

*Be the innocence
that dissolves all walls
and invites all hearts.*

A WALL OR A BRIDGE

The question is simple: In any given situation, will I choose to be a wall or a bridge? To be indifferent takes absolutely no effort. You maintain the status quo and don't get a speck closer to those around you. To be vulnerable, on the other hand, takes being aware how those self-defended walls are hurting you and everyone else.

In high school I developed an edgy manner. I would hurl clever and cutting words at my macho buddies. My inner hurt got a justified pleasure, as stupid as it sounds. My bros soon picked up on the attitude and flung it back at me. Ooo, that smarted. I understood what I was doing and stopped in a hurry. The mirror they held up to me quickly bore fruits. I was soon able to confide in one of my friends about a relationship in which I had gotten hurt. I easily could have put up the wall, blamed her, and supposedly saved face. I wouldn't settle for that. I knew building bridges into my own heart was the way I had to go.

Emotional walls eventually crumble, and where they were bridges appear. Being a stolid, immovable grump is not really you anyway; kind thoughts and gestures are, and they have true power—that's why people respond to them. The precedent was set over 2,000 years ago by a man who epitomized what a bridge can be. Despite enduring the anathema of the ages, he forgave. You, too, can do it. Your mission might be to ease off being sarcastic and ease into being the nice one. You don't have to sound spiritual or gush with the mushy stuff; a sincere "Hello, how are you?" will do. Observe how a few kind words make you feel.

If a simple greeting and pleasantry is too difficult don't worry, just smile and nod.

Two priceless examples on New York City subways taught me what a true bridge is. In neither was a word exchanged. In the first incident, a woman got on the subway cradling a young child in her arms. Nothing unusual there. You see it all the time on the subways. I happened to look over at them. I could see other passengers turn their heads too and smile. Some stood to offer their seats. The subway car softened like the natural thaw of spring. You know who was the bridge—not us subterranean New Yorkers who sat looking straight ahead with our indifferent, protective stares, but a gentle babe with no turf to defend, no agendas, no pain to hide.

Right then I realized where true power lies: in purity and innocence. We hardened New Yorkers were surely disarmed.

The next thaw appeared the night a huge Caribbean woman stepped into the subway car. Before she could grab the pole for support, the subway car jerked forward. She fell backwards, crashing to the floor. Her surprised scream filled the car and then segued right into full-bodied accents of pure joy and laughter. All of us smiled and cracked up with her. She didn't mind either. Her childlike honesty had snapped us out of our guarded facades into our true, warm selves.

Once again, disarmed by innocence.

See how easy it can be. See how the pure in heart, just by being themselves, are bridges. They are simple-hearted folk that you'd pass right by and probably wouldn't notice. Yet once that innocence touches you, it's meltdown time. That's proof; that's power. They offer a way out. They help break down a belief that a stone-cold wall is a wall at all.

My opportunity to be a bridge happened when I was working at a school. Because the school was based on a holistic concept of man I expected most employees, especially ones in positions of authority, to readily share smiles or hellos when I passed them in the halls.

Well, that often wasn't the case, which made no sense to me. How can they not even smile, I wondered? I would walk by, smile, and get literally nothing out of them. My mind took it a step further when the same kept happening: If I were their boss, I mused, I would seriously challenge this kind of attitude. Where is their friendliness? Is this a loving way to treat co-workers?

I was perplexed, annoyed, but kept a ready smile whenever I walked by them.

Then I realized: I have no idea what's actually going on inside them. They could be full of troubles and cannot reach out. This wasn't an excuse for their continual coolness but it led to a greater realization: On some level, on some very basic level, they are hurting! They don't need me being upset or judging them, they need love. They need me to be a bridge, whether they know it or not.

That's what I became. Every time we passed I either smiled or greeted them if they happened to look. It didn't matter if they responded. My bridge was intact, operational, and ready for them to cross over at any time.

DIVINE DEEPENING

What does offering goodwill cost you
versus the cost of protecting your heart?

Never dismiss a coincidence.
The Universe and your heart
are syncing up and confirming,
You are on the right path.

COINCIDENCES, NOT ACCIDENTS

Have you ever thought about someone before going to the supermarket and then run into them in the produce section? Maybe you wondered what happened to an old high school friend and then they friend you on Facebook? At one time or another everyone experiences coincidences. In my mind, they are less like anomalies and more like the confluence of heartfelt living and life.

On a train in southern Bavaria (Germany) many years ago I walked by a family and thought I recognized the son. I stopped and asked him if he attended Connecticut College, the school I was at. He said, Yes. We had a short exchange and parted ways. Less than a month later I moved into Harkness, a college dorm, for my sophomore year and there on the same floor three doors down was Karl, the guy I had met on the train.

Was my experience just a coincidence? An act of a capricious God? The stars lining up for us lucky ones? Here's what Webster says about the word *coincide*, the root word of coincidence: 1. to occupy the same place in space or time. 2. to correspond in nature, character, or function. 3. to be in accord or agreement.

His definitions make it plain (at least to me) that to dismiss these events as the workings of an accidental universe makes worse sense. They point to a more intentional design, even a lining up and fulfilling of desires that brings us together with someone or something.

I've participated in enough coincidences to know that: 1. I am playing my part, be it conscious or unconscious, 2. The coincidence manifests good, and 3. It often is some want being fulfilled. This last point was clearly illustrated in my Lower East Side New York apartment.

I had a spare room in my railroad flat that I used as a healing room. Because French doors opened from it into the front room overlooking the street, I felt that the room needed more privacy. A long curtain in front of the French doors would do the trick. My first step was measuring the length of the wall, including the doors. It totaled 128 inches. Being thrifty I decided to go out on the streets and look for a curtain rod. Heck, this was New York, you never knew what people might throw away.

Did I pray about this? No. Did I ask divine Intelligence for help? Not consciously. I knew what I needed and headed out on to the streets to find it.

I walked east from my Ninth Street and Second Avenue apartment. Before reaching the corner at First Avenue I spotted a long, metal spring tension curtain rod sticking out of someone's garbage. Seems about right, I thought. I brought it back to my apartment and opened it up. Its full length measured 128.75 inches, almost exactly what I needed! My girlfriend made the curtain. That was that.

Were my biorhythms peaking on that day? Who knows. Why that particular day, anyway? Did my expectation of good manifest the rod? Was it my trust? Something in the universe surely lined up for me.

A different type of coincidence sprang out of necessity. One day I took my car to be repaired. My wife dropped me at work. Around five as I was packing up to leave, I realized I had no way home, unless I stayed late for my wife to come. Instead, I gathered my things and headed to leave. I had hitchhiked halfway around the world years ago, how hard could it be to get the nine miles home. As I walked down the hall toward the exit, I had the thought that God knows all my needs. I felt more confident.

I walked out the door. Waiting at the curbside to pick up her daughter was Louise, the mother of one of my daughter's classmates. She also was the only parent in the school I was aware of who lived past us in the same direction. I went straight to her car, asked her, and I was on the way home.

Similarly, months later following our family's move closer to work I confidently used the same tack when our car was at the garage again: I walked out the front door. No one was waiting there, so I walked down the sidewalk trusting everything would work out. I was no more than thirty yards down the sidewalk when Chris, a fellow employee, drove up next to me and asked if I needed a ride home. Of course.

How do I explain the ease of getting each ride? I was listening and doing my part and the all-knowing, all-providing divine Orchestrator arranged the rest.

The incident that inspired this article was a return visit to Stonington, Connecticut, a picturesque, former Portuguese fishing village, not far from the Rhode Island border. I had lived there right out of college in a grand Federal-style home at 1 Main Street. Except for the modest twentieth-century houses that packed the point, the rest of the village was comprised of original Colonial structures dating back to the 1700s and elegant Federal period homes of the 1800s.

During my summer stay in the village I had the fortune of hearing one of America's foremost poets, James Merrill, read a poem of his at the Stonington

Free Library. Merrill, like other writers from New York, came up the coast to camp out unnoticed in Stonington village and write.

In this case, he had spun the old RCA Victor records' dog, Nipper*, right off the 33 1/3 lp into a poem of erudite proportions. His literary sophistication had my intellect spinning about as fast as the dog he had appropriated off the RCA label. I left impressed but unsure why. We'll get back to Merrill.

Fast forward twenty years and change. My family and mother-in-law were visiting Stonington. While my wife and her mother shopped Stonington's main drag, my son and I ambled the side streets in the heart of the village. As we turned onto a tiny street inside a white picket fence a man was repairing the clapboards on a house. We stopped to chat. The house he was working on, he told me, was owned by a famous writer from New York named McClatchy. He added that McClatchy wrote for a magazine. I'd never heard of him. As the man methodically went about his repair, he proudly stated that he took care of seven homes in the village. He liked his work and, I could tell, appreciated my interest.

After giving a blow by blow of one of his larger renovations in the village, he got into family stuff. He was from a large Portuguese family just outside the village.

That made sense given the long history of the Portuguese in Stonington. He said his name was Billy Paul. The face behind the weather-etched facial lines and dirty blond hair rang with familiarity: "I remember you from New London," I said. "We moved there from North Stonington," he told me. When I got around to my name, he said that his sister Doris knew an Ann DeGange (my oldest sister who we call Betsy). "That's my sister," I replied. I recalled his sister, too. We got a charge out of the coincidental connection. We shook hands and departed.

I couldn't wait to tell my sister of my encounter with Billy Paul.

My family stopped in the neighboring town of Mystic for the summer art festival and then headed back to my dad's house. On the mantle in the living room was an article from the New London Day, the local newspaper, that had been saved by Betsy for me with a note saying she thought I'd enjoy the article because of my love of writing. I opened the newspaper. Staring out at me from behind the office desk of his Stonington home, which I had stood in front of an hour earlier, was Sandy McClatchy, the New York writer.

I read on. "Sandy McClatchy, one of the most powerful and controversial writers of our time, editor of poetry journals, The New Yorker magazine, self-designated keeper of literary standards, and literary heir to James Merrill, his mentor from Yale University." *James Merrill,* whoa, I couldn't have dreamt up this one if I tried.

Bless Billy and Betsy, James and Sandy and the gift of listening.

I wrote to McClatchy of being at his house, the article, and hearing James Merrill years earlier. His response: "Coincidence shapes our lives, and we shape coincidence." I'll keep following my heart.

*Nipper was a terrier that became famous from a painting titled "His Master's Voice," which eventually was used as the logo for RCA Victor records, a well-known record label popular from the early 1930s through the 1960s.

DIVINE DEEPENING
Recall an incident where life perfectly lined up for you. Exactly what did you do to co-create this?
Keep doing it.

As I let go, I let life

DEATH AS A WAY OF LIFE

A way of life, death? You're probably thinking, Can I take a bye on this one? Not to worry, Supreme Intelligence has given us the helmet of understanding by which to go out on the playing field and tackle death itself. I know it sounds daunting, but it is doable. Can death really touch you? No. You were made to last forever—at least the real part of you, your spiritual identity. What is my authority for such a claim? The meat of my own experience.

Should I rely on anyone else's seeing through the veil, or victory over the "last enemy" death? As much as I've studied the words and works of Christian, Buddhist, Indian and other spiritual masters and have strived to follow, my enlightenment rests solely on my own realizations. They did their work. Their victories are theirs. We rejoice over the blessings they brought and faith they inspire. My victory, though, must come from my walk through life. Otherwise, I'm spouting timeless platitudes, which may be as true as can be, but don't have the substance and proof backing them.

There are those times of grace (like the time my daughter was born) when our surrendered state of being gets touched by wisdom direct from Source.

Think about the way you were as a very young child. That's all I did the day I mused upon who I am—my spirit of helping out, my unsettled nature, my disdain for limits, my love of both stillness and movement, and so on. I saw how the world had tried to make me believe these qualities came from and were molded by my parents, by growing up, by the environment, and by everything outside of me. In a flash of insight, I understood that they were there from the time I could remember myself as a child. They had been refined or morphed some since then. But who I was, my individuality or soul, was intact from day one. I knew I had come in with it. It was already mine. My individuality predated my family and my life as Mark.

Recall Jesus' words "Before Abraham was, I am." This would be nonsensical if he was referring to the human personality born of Mary. He was pointing to his real nature, the eternal Christ, which surely existed before Abraham the man. I, too, knew that my true qualities, which could be likened to a permanent personality, were already there and untouched by this one life.

A wholly different realization came when I was thinking about my body. The idea wasn't a big number. In fact, I can't believe everyone on the planet doesn't have the very same thoughts on occasion, they're so basic: *If my spirit were to go away, flee the premises* (my body) *so to speak, my body would drop like a life-less sack to the ground.* In other words, without me my body is a heap of flesh. This sounds ridiculously obvious, yet the tangible clarity of it in my mind was as real as the distinction between a living tree and a dried, dead limb that has fallen from it to the ground. My spirit—the vitality of thoughts and feelings consti-tuting my identity—is the animating part of me that goes on, even if the body is discarded. (A couple of very vivid out-of-body experiences around this time confirmed the sense that I wasn't my physical body.)

There you have it—the front and back ends of my life covered. Now back to the title, "Death as a Way of Life". The title sounds contradictory, given that I've just posited that every life has a pre-existence and an eternal spiritual nature that lives on past the dropping of the physical body. Why then does living need death at all? If I am, I am. Period.

Consider again my two realizations: I let go of tra-ditional ideas of my mortal identity I had taken for granted and allowed new views to come forth. Isn't that a form of death? Rather than being locked into a world view of myself, I yielded. The pictures of life I carried (I'll call them mortally mental impositions.) died and made room for expansive views of myself that resonated true in me.

Every second, I am giving up something in order to move on. If I am sitting in a chair rewriting this and get hungry, then I must get up and go to the kitchen for food. My comfortable, dear friend, the chair, has to be let go of.

Learning is the same. If a teacher shows you a better and quicker way of solving a problem, then it's wise to discard the old system to make life easier. You are letting in more intelligence by letting go of a traditional way of doing things. It is sloughing off a part of yourself. That's a good death.

On the contrary, if your ego steps in and convinces you not to accept this person's teaching because of their race, sex, accent, or the fact they have more degrees than you, then you have missed an opportunity to come into more life, and instead have died in your own prejudices. That's a wrongful death.

Is the idea of death anything to be afraid of when more and more life awaits?

DIVINE DEEPENING

What beliefs in security are you holding to
that if you released then life might open in
ways you could never dream of?
Dare yourself to go there.

Being still, you behold.

OH WOW! LEONIDS IS BACK IN TOWN

"Look at that . . . ," "Oh wow!" "Did you see . . . ," erupt in awe and trail off into the night sky. But don't look too intently, you'll miss the quick flit flash off to the right.

Leonids* and his shower of meteor beauties are back in town for a one-night stand. I must warn you, standing and craning your neck upward is not going to work. Gazing up from the supine is far more neck friendly, especially at three o'clock in the morning.

So stretch the mat, lay out flat, and begin your watch, not knowing (and that's the fun) where you must wing your eyes to grab a fleeting streak, a fiery tail, a tantalizing white-whoosh-and-it's-gone.

Scientists explain meteor showers as hot burning minerals and dust meeting Earth's atmosphere only to be snuffed out. Accurate it may be, but how dry. Did I bring my army mat out in the middle of the night to think of meteoroid death? No way. I came out to be dazzled. I came out to behold the universe. In short, to gaze past the physics of my nose into wonderment.

And Leonids delivered. Brilliantly charged seconds lit up my man-turned-boy face and kept it at a child's edge of awe for over an hour.

We are like those meteoric lights blazing across the sky. We stream through the world for an instant, allowing others to behold our stunning splendor. Then we dissolve and are transformed into finer etheric light (as Tesla understood) not into darkness nor oblivion.

*Leonids is the name for the spectacular meteor showers that radiate in the sky from where the constellation Leo is and that were scientifically recognized in 1833 and continue to the present usually peaking around November 18.

DIVINE DEEPENING

What wonder, beauty, magic, and mystery
of creation are you letting pass by
because you are so mesmerized by your programs?
Please stop, behold, and be awed.

MEDITATION

Grace and Ease

Isn't where I am the most perfect place I can be? Isn't it the right place at the right time, if only I perceive it so? Perceiving this reality is a gift of Grace. And it is continual, not a onetime event. The key is to position our hearts. Let's hop into the flow and be the ease of Grace.

Ease your body into the right place, the right posture. Ease into your breath. Ease into your beautiful heart. Ease out of excessive thoughts and emotions. Let them be. Let them dissolve.

Recall a moment from the past where you were incredibly at one, where things flowed effortlessly, where you were alive and fully invested, yet were like a witness to the harmony around you. Exactly where were you? Let this experience be yours now. Taste the atmosphere, the people, the action at hand. Notice how the whole thing happens in ease. Feel it with your whole being. How is your heart? How does your body respond? Be aware. Don't overthink it. Live it. Let the happiness and harmony of that

experience fill you. Let your senses overflow
with joy and contentment. Just take it all in and
do nothing. Find eternity in the gift Grace offers
you.

When ready and with closed eyes, bring all
the feelings, sensations, and deep contentment
into the present where you sit, and into your
body. Savor the Grace of what you recalled.
Know that it lives in you, and always will. You can
tap into it any time. It's your very own reservoir
of Grace.

When you open your eyes, allow your inner
harmony to be one with the environment around
you. Stay there for a minute or two as you integrate the experience. Let Grace move you forward in greater ease with life.

8
CHAPTER

THE
JOURNEY
HOME

MARK LECLAIR DEGANGE

Spreading my divine roots
is enough.

THE ROYAL WAY

In his footsteps is marked
A proven way,
Life, Truth, and Love

Why go down an unblessed
Path the world's way
His is straight above

What glint has gold
When Life makes bold
                Its goodness peerless bright

How lisp all lies
When Truth descries
                The glory of the Light

What hold has hate
When Love's estate
                Is all-embracing might

Why fawn on fame
When lives his name
        Heralding life aright

        It's clear in Christ
        I won't delay.

DIVINE DEEPENING

Does the road you walk bless your life
in the highest possible way? If not,
what should your next steps be?

Is your Comfort Zone
- *A sense of stagnation—don't want to move because I am used to lazy me.*
- *A limit—doing as much as possible and now I am reaching my fear point*
- *Freedom—living in the 'unknown' as I allow Spirit to blaze the way.*

CRANE VISTAS

One day at the end of our acting workshop in the Ansonia Hotel, Dick and his wife, Beryl, (my acting coaches) asked us to bring in and embody a mechanical structure we chose from Manhattan's streets. I chose a building crane as my piece. At our next meeting I lay on the floor and did certain movements with my legs to effect the crane arm and cab and made creaking and grinding, metallic sounds with my voice. Dick broke out in a gleeful smile.

When I stood up next to him I told him, this one is right down at Lincoln Center, and is bigger than big. He related that he once had climbed a crane that was nine or ten stories. Next thing out of my mouth was, *You wanna do it?* He nodded like a kid.

Now I had an excuse: I was a juiced-up, twenty-six-year-old male actor, living my dream in New York, New York, who grew up climbing any tree in sight, including the giant spruce in my grandmother's driveway. Bring it on. But Dick—a tall, brittle-looking and awkward-moving, Actors' Studio vet just north of 60, with a "Wild Bill" Hickok mane of white hair and a quirky, bent smile under his white mustache—what was he doing climbing cranes? He was game beyond crazy, and I loved him for it.

Just before midnight Dick and I met on a side street at Lincoln Center between Broadway and Amsterdam. We huddled next to the massive treads of the crane for a minute, each not sure about our next move.

As I peeked out at the night watchman one way, Dick, unnoticed, walked quietly around the crane the opposite way. Next thing I heard was the tapping of feet moving across the deck of the crane's cab. *Oh my, it must be Dick. Time to go*. I raced around the side, hopped up on deck, shot the night watchman in the trailer a glance—who fortunately didn't notice a thing—and moved toward the massive, red, metal arm that rose into the night.

Dick already was moving up the arm's inner scaffold. His wiry, bent arms and legs, juxtaposed against the slick metal geometry, made him look out of place. Doesn't matter, I thought, just climb.

We wasted no time leaving the construction trailer well below. Once we were a few stories up, no one around would bother us. New Yorkers are too concerned with what's happening on ground level, especially after midnight.

Higher and higher, Dick with his bony, gangly frame and hair flowing in the night, and me with my smaller, flexible frame keeping pace. I was impressed he could climb so dexterously. The early stages of the climb were an exciting forward quest into the sky though somewhat slow because of the larger distances and angles between the metal tubes we had to hoist our bodies onto.

Rapidly we were gaining the heights. He was facing away from me on the inside of the arm. I could see him, but couldn't tell how he was doing. We weren't talking, just acting, as actors do. We passed the ten-story mark, Dick's previous record.

At about thirteen or fourteen stories up Dick stopped. He turned around toward me to say he had had a night. As he headed down I assured him we would make it all the way. Knowing what he had accomplished I didn't want to let him down.

The task ahead felt huge being now alone. I refused to look up or down. The bars right in front of my eyes were the only place I needed to be. My eyes, hands, feet, and thoughts were locked into super focus with each movement. There could be no slips.

I accelerated my climbing. The crane arm was narrowing every minute, presenting shorter spaces to negotiate and more metal against my body. I welcomed the solidness at such heights.

Nearing the upper sections of the crane two new challenges appeared: An extremely greasy cable as thick as my forearm emerged out of the inner arm. I did not want to get my hands greasy. Yet I had to climb right over it. The other issue was the ever-increasing sway factor. I felt the crane arm moving me through the air, not too much, but enough to make me nervously tighten my hold on the metal.

Finally, with the metal arm not much wider than the length of my hand, I was at the top. The clock near Columbus Circle read quarter of one. Forty-five minutes and it was ours. I hugged the top and yelled our victory. I was euphoric.

I counted the floors of a building on Broadway. At about the thirty-third floor I felt I was eye level.

A fantastic panorama of Columbus Circle and the southern end of Central Park lay below. Except for a lamplight here and there all was asleep in the park. North, straddling and seemingly stranded over the Hudson River like a great sailing ship of the night, rose the George Washington Bridge with its lit-up suspension. Looking west past the river's reflection of the shimmering city lights, I took in the Palisades and pockets of New Jersey towns as far as I could see.

I had won these celestial views. I wanted to savor the victory.

But the wind had kicked up and the swaying was for real. My body draped over the narrow metal arm on both sides. I rode through space thrilled to my wits. What if the arm were to break, I thought. Got to let that thought go. I took my first and only look straight down the crane arm to see what I faced next. My stomach grimaced. God help me. I cannot slip.

I flicked my sneakers off. I wanted to feel every bar against my feet. Slowly, real slowly, I began my descent. I tenaciously made extra sure of each foot plant and hand hold. There was no margin of error, just the next bar to cling to. I stuck to that one single task as I backed myself downwards

Up had been all adventure, conquest. Down was strictly about my life.

When the bottom finally came, Dick was waiting and we exulted like satisfied warriors.

Why do a crazy stunt like this? Was I defying authority? Looking for a challenge because life is too boring? Not really—I only wanted to climb a crane. It was there to be done. And the right person (Dick) was there who shared my passion for going higher.

I didn't yet know that sitting down and turning inward could take me much, much higher. So, I climbed things, hiked mountains, ran marathons, and spun myself into as many pirouettes as possible. The point was to leap into each metaphor with joy and take it to the limit.

DIVINE DEEPENING

Can anything really stop you except
the heart that got you this far?
Your heart is already victorious.
Can you credit it as so?

Are you in willful dis-grace
of pursuing what destroys
and missing the living grace
of realizing what upholds?

THE JAVELIN, THE GREENHOUSE, AND THE NEW MAN

The apostle Paul in one of his letters talked about "putting off the old man," or getting rid of your old habits. A simple analogy is to stop wearing clothes that don't fit. Why hold on to a version of ourselves that only restricts? The past can be like a ball and chain, as an old blues song by Janis Joplin put it, and we often end up dragging it behind us like a child pulling their worn-out safety blanket around the house.

There came a time when I dropped "the old man" in favor of a more spiritualized life, or the new man.

When I was in high school and college, I thought of myself as someone who did what was right, told the truth, and was responsible. But, my sense of right and wrong somehow had morphed into an "it's-no-big-deal" moral numbness. This especially pertained to how I treated others' property.

An instance of this occurred during high school. My friends and I on occasion would have informal track competitions: running, jumping, and throwing the shot put. Usually, these Saturday events took place near or at the United States Coast Guard Academy practice fields in our hometown. During one of these events on Coast Guard property, I found a javelin lying around and was psyched that it was an international regulation-sized one. I decided to take it. I was not the type who walked off with something that wasn't mine. I honestly can't remember anything else I ever took. I simply wanted it. The javelin ended up in my parents' attic—out of sight and out of mind.

Years passed. On one of my trips to my parents' house I began thinking about the javelin I'd stolen. I knew I should return it, but I dismissed the thought and returned to New York. But the thought of that stolen javelin wouldn't leave me alone.

On a subsequent trip to my parent's home, I pulled the javelin out of the attic, borrowed the VW Bug, and headed for the Coast Guard Academy. At the entrance an impeccably dressed cadet came out of the gatehouse and asked where I was going (with a long javelin sticking out the driver's side window!). Without thinking I simply answered, "I'm going to the field house to return the javelin." He was completely disarmed and waved me through. Honesty had been my passport. When I put the javelin down in the field house and walked out, I felt as if a burden had been lifted.

The second instance where a willful numbness overcame what was right occurred the night our dorm basketball team won the college intramural championship. We celebrated at a local tavern, came back to campus, partied, and headed to the college greenhouse. I climbed onto its glass roof to see if campus security were in their gatehouse. Near the top, I must have stepped squarely onto a glass pane. The glass shattered under me. As I whirled around to get off, pane after pane shattered beneath me. Only metal blinds prevented me from falling into the greenhouse and badly hurting myself. I jumped off, and my friends and I hightailed it for the arboretum across the road to hide.

College officials knew guys from our dorm had done it. Threats of expulsion were in the air. None of us (especially me) had the courage to come forward, and we escaped with no consequences. A couple of years later I graduated, and memories of the greenhouse faded. As time went by, I began to see that my desire to know the Truth would leave no stone unturned when it came to facing past misdeeds. Things I didn't necessarily like about myself were coming to the surface to be cleared away. I understood it takes humility and obedience to own up to something. Humility is the yielding required to face the music; obedience is the act of following through to correct the situation. Being lawful becomes a natural expression of living.

About Jesus it was said: ". . . he swerved not, well knowing that to obey the divine order and trust God, saves retracing and traversing anew the path from sin to holiness."*

My inevitable "retracing" came unexpectedly. A few decades after the greenhouse incident, the thought came one day, *You have to pay the college back for the greenhouse.* I knew the thought was dead on, and I surrendered without a flinch. I remembered the name of the local glass company in my college town (it also was my hometown) that did the repairs and called them to see what it would cost to make such a repair today. Within a short time I'd written a substantial check and sent it to the college, earmarking it for the facilities department. I felt a quiet sense of completion as if I'd closed a chapter in my life.

As I act more and more from my heart's integrity anything and everything unlike it gets churned up to be dealt with. This can tempt me to identify myself by behaviors that miss the mark. In reality, they are like displaced children inside me needing to be loved and set on the right path. Then, the world and I are both safeguarded.

* Eddy, *Science and Health,* 20.

DIVINE DEEPENING

If your soul depended on it (and it does)
who must you make an "at-one-ment" with?
What actions will you take?

If I lose myself in an activity,
what have I lost—
separation
effort
time—
essentially nothing.
What have I gained—
oneness
fulfillment
eternity—
essentially my life.

DISHWASHING YOUR WAY TO NIRVANA OR TAKING THE GRUDGE OUT OF ZEN

While living in Manhattan's Lower East Side, my girlfriend and I had a couple over for lunch at her apartment. When we finished eating, the man offered to do the dishes, stating that he felt a Zen-like oneness while dishwashing. I'm sorry to say that a cynical voice reared up in me and said, *I've got to see this*. I had a mixed taste in my mouth about this tortured poet-triathlete whose first greeting to me months earlier had been a kick in the sole of my foot as he stood there and asked me how fast I had run the marathon. At the time, I was sitting on a blanket on the sidewalk at St. Mark's Place and First Avenue next to my future girlfriend (his ex).

He bared his tightly strung muscular arms, hunched himself over the small sink Quasimodo-like (something was wrong with this picture already), thrust his pile drivers into a stack of dishes, and started working those babies hard. *Why such intensity and concentration?* I wondered. *Did we eat with Crazy Glue or something?* I watched his concealed angst pour out onto the defenseless plates—and prayed none of them would break.

I, too, am still washing dishes. Had I thought that at this stage of life I would be liberated of the task? Didn't happen. I'm thankful for it. (I also hope I'm not as critical of others' Zen aspirations.) *Thankful* for washing dishes? Not exactly. Finally, I am getting the right feel for it. Meaning, I no longer resent the time I spend scraping the scraps off.

Just keeping my mind focused on washing the dishes can be a big job. First there's the gorgeous view of the distant mountains (wish I was there). Then there's the inner stuff: *Dishes again! I could be doing . . .* or *I'm too good to waste my time.* I've probably whined my way through the gamut of uncomely complaints and not even realized it. I'm still washing, and grateful for the next opportunity to be present.

It feels as if I'm washing myself away, that is, cleaning my dirty stack of resentments, judgments, and whatever else I harbor inside until I'm given to the task without hesitation or inner drama, and—especially for those getting into a spiritual thing—without thinking that I am doing Karma Yoga or Swarma Yoga. What I am doing is the dishes.

One evening when doing the dishes alone, a simple realization came: I was washing the dishes with care and attention so that Maria and the children could eat off clean plates. As basic as this may sound, I felt a sense of illumination and joy shoot through me. I had found nirvana at my fingertips.

Of course, I prefer the dishwasher.

DIVINE DEEPENING
Out of your myriad daily do's which one
is most lacking your undivided Zen?

Misconceptions put the blinders on.
Just blink. Love is right next to you.

LOVING DUTY

While living in Greece in the 1990s, I married a lovely Athenian woman. I discovered that my commitment to her included the land, the food, the language, the holidays, and especially her son, Georgie.

I first met five-year-old Georgie in his mother's bed and bath shop. He was playing animatedly by himself behind the cash register, waving a coin in the air, then settling into a quietly plaintive Greek song. I was charmed. I also saw he was blind. Nonetheless, he and I went for a walk that very day.

I soon learned that my wife's friends had her story backward. All they saw was a single mom with a blind son—and a difficult, tainted life ahead. When I came along those friends were swift to remind her how lucky she was to have *gotten* me, as if I was the American knight come to the rescue. She quietly bore it, while I felt angry at their blindness. I was the blessed one: In one swoop, I had gotten two loves who readily accepted and loved me.

Yet an instant family and instant responsibilities, besides the language barrier, showed me I had so much to learn. My spiritual practice at the time, akin to a martial arts meditation, had brought balance and more peace in my life, but it hadn't taught me to truly love. The love I expressed felt more like a vow of spiritual labor.

In those days, I needed support from all quarters, both earthly and heavenly. The words of one of my guides, Padre Pio—"Duty before . . . something holy"— came as a solace. The something holy in my eyes was the meditation I taught. Duty, on the other hand, was the parenting. Why I didn't see caring for Georgie as something holy was a lapse of heart. His need for help with virtually all he did—eating, bathing, getting from place to place—weighed me down and got the better of me. My patience would fizzle out. I'd react, followed by tearful remorse. Georgie deserved more, and I knew it.

My cries to God seemed to go nowhere. I felt far from the spiritual mastery I was seeking. Aren't we made to love, I thought. What would it take for me to get it? What it took was a clearer sense of God and man that dawned in me in my study of the Christ Science. A universal God of love was revealed to me, which made infinite sense. My wife and children felt Love's embrace, also. My vow of spiritual labor began to fade and "the unlabored motion of divine energy"* began to appear.

I can't say I shed all the old ways overnight. But I was set straight about 'duty.' The burdened dutiful sense of caring for my son had lost its grip on me. After all, who was the real father here? Not the personal me, but divine Love itself, which was helping me bear my load more gracefully. When tension would try to get the best of me, I started relinquishing my personal control and recognizing God's control.

Life with Georgie went from me telling him, to me listening more to him. The biggest key was replacing my need to make incessant corrections about posture, eating, walking, and organizing, with the understanding I've gained that he is endowed from above with the intelligence to master all these things. Doing so helped me to *love more* and *parent less*. By simply being there for Georgie, I earned more of his trust. He began to open up and share his personal challenges.

Our times together became more fun! He loves to laugh and he enjoys wordplay. I do too. I would make up funny Greek-English equivalencies, or joke about his grammatical choices in English, or my own poor Greek pronunciation.

Then, when it was time to help him learn unfamiliar routes, like the ones he traveled on his college campus, I would suggest a course correction or two, and check to be sure he was secure where he was heading. Above all, I learned to trust the divine Presence to keep both him and me straight on the path.

*Eddy, *Science and Health,* 445.

DIVINE DEEPENING

What gift of God are you grappling with,
which if you altered your sorry attitude,
would become the blessing it truly is?

It's a crime to stick anything after "I am" other than well-being.

CALLING ALL SUPERHEROES

Superheroes live in our midst. In our minds, anyway, thanks to Marvel Comics and Hollywood. Superheroes are the rage, flying and leaping about saving the planet from darkness. They inspire with their fight for what's right as much as by their cool super powers.

You emerge from the movies somehow hoping that one day you'll wake up and find yourself able to give your body a silent command and suddenly be on a rooftop (okay, maybe that's my fantasy).

Don't be surprised if it's reported that someone out there actually is doing mighty acts of benevolence like our superheroes. Isn't it only a matter of opening to what's possible? An old friend who has about as much honesty and integrity as any man I ever knew told me a story witnessed by a scientist friend of his of an astronaut who had just returned from the moon and was on the examination table. As he leaped off the table and hit the floor, he bounced up close to the ceiling—before remembering that he was on Earth and subject to its gravity.

If we suspend disbelief for a second, what was that about?

The mind's power. When we are able to overcome the mind's subservience to so-called natural laws so much more is possible. Jesus, Nityananda of Ganeshpuri, Satya Sai Baba, Mary Baker Eddy, and Padre Pio (to name a few) benevolently demonstrated man's power of healing and manifestation. Are their proofs of divine Presence possible for us, too?

What I have seen is that more and more people are awakening and aligning themselves with the understanding of their perfection and wholeness, which fosters the reality of faster healings and the removal of physical barriers and takes the lid off the universe of possibilities. I myself have witnessed instantaneous healings and manifestations. The challenge is staying firmly planted in the realm of the affirmative and possible. The media and the movies would make us believe that darkness (the negation of life) also has real power. To be honest, who hasn't been tempted by the negating side of life at one time or another.

While in high school I had a summer job at the post office. One day I faked sickness to get out of work. Like an actor I started convincing myself I was getting ill, i.e., walking slowly, talking weakly, imagining I was fluish, the whole bit. Before long I actually felt that way. My request was granted. I headed for the door, victorious and unwell.

I would say it took over 15 minutes to overcome the lie I had devised in the first place.

This was mastery over the body in the wrong way. What real power does a cold, a flu, or any diseased condition have over us, except our willingness to believe we are subject to such things? What if we made an unwavering, mental protest at the first symptoms of a stomachache. Could the stomach resist? Does it have a mind of its own to talk back and promote aches and pains? What if we loved our stomach unconditionally then and there, meaning, whatever was going on in it, we flood those ill feelings with the TNT of TLC.

The empowering of anything and everything deleterious to man's health and well-being is the Pandora's box of the ages. I believe open season on man will remain until he claims that these conditions have no power over him.

I witnessed an example familiar to all while living in a fourth-floor walk-up in the Lower East Side of Manhattan years ago. My neighbors across the hall were a Polish couple. She was a housewife and he a retired American Airlines mechanic. From what I could tell, both were healthy, although she was the more vital one, going up and down stairs, shopping, conversing with her neighbors. Him you rarely saw.

One day after being neighbors a few years, I realized she was no longer there. She had passed away. The few times I saw him shortly afterwards he appeared withdrawn and sunken in spirit. His only comments were about missing her. I regret not reaching out more than I did. A month or so after, he passed on.

This is not a unique story. The December 23, 2016 version of DailyMail.com carried a story of a couple married 64 years from Tennessee who died hours apart. CBS News (Jan. 26, 2017) reported a New Hyde Park, N.Y. couple married for 70 years also passing away hours apart. I find these stories analogous to my post office story, only with permanent consequences. To my knowledge my neighbor didn't possess spiritual powers different than you or me. Through his thought-desire-will he turned off the juice to his body and moved on to be with her. He made his choice, and was demonstrating his power over the body.

What will our choice be? To bow down to limitation and illness. Why not act more like superheroes and affirm our powers of life? Why not expose our penchant for dis-eased states and unhealthy lifestyles for what they really are, empowerment in the wrong direction? Lovingly lift that child (your well-being) from the precipice of ignorance and impositions and see it leap over that challenge in a single bound.

DIVINE DEEPENING

Have you ever dismissed an extraordinary
event—a manifestation, a sudden healing,
a synchronicity—as a fluke or pure luck?
What if Spirit was working directly with you?
What if you could tune into this Power regularly?
What if you and It were really one?

MARK LECLAIR DEGANGE

Am I choosing the fastest way home?

CORRECTION ON I-95 SOUTH

The correction was staring straight at me. I could have deflected it and pretended it was nothing. No, I was too aware. I would not let it go. I had just finished claiming the truth of this woman's health as I dropped her off. I would not allow such an obvious attempt of my ego to slip by and leave me okay with being unconscious.

When the woman first walked toward my car I tried not to stare. Bright pink two-piece sweats with her belly spilling out generously front and side, and a tattoo declaring her birth sign blazed across the top of her chest. Her long black, braided hair going sideways, back, and to the front of her body added to her unkempt appearance.

Okay, Mark, just do your job. We left and I drove her to her doctor's appointment.

An hour later she was in my car again as we drove north towards her apartment in the projects. She related how the drug therapy for her damaged knee seemed to be going nowhere. I turned the conversation towards more inspired things and I could feel her become hopeful that she could have a better life. When I dropped her off she said something about my business card, "Heart-centered Energy healing," had attracted her. She mentioned being shot and now being fearful of going outside at night to her car. She also mentioned her sickly adult daughter and wondered if I could help her. Twice she promised to call me. I was touched.

About halfway back on I-95 South I suddenly thought, *the paint can!* I had left the unopened gallon of paint I was going to return to Sherwin-Williams on the back seat right next to the client. I twisted my head hard to the right to look in back. (Of course, the can was right there.) My upper body jerked, too, and the car swerved right. I quickly straightened it out. The real correction, though, was crystal clear as I drove down the interstate, and I grabbed onto it like a dog onto a bone and refused to let it go: The crooked places of my thought needed to be made straight, there and then. A total stranger in a state of weakness and with hope minutes before had confided in me and in return my lame ego somehow how conjured her acting like a thief with my paint can—and she had walked slowly and with a cane. What was I thinking? Even if I was picking up on something in a shadowy past of hers, the issue was mine. Did I want to make it my own?

When my mind (the egoistic one) steers my heart sideways, I get put away and life goes askew. Crashes happen. Painful detours down unwanted byways happen. Separation from the good (the woman) in front of me happens, and the door opens for hell to walk through.

I must choose my heart first, and trust it to move me forward.

DIVINE DEEPENING

Is your ego slyly pointing to an error in another as a way of covering up your own? Could the error be yours only? Deeper yet, could it be a lie about you?

Home is wherever I am.

YOU ARE HOME

If I could plant one thought in the heart and mind of every person on earth it would be this: You are home in love.

I read a statement in *THE ARCHKO VOLUME** about Jesus to the effect that as he walked in the hills of Israel even wild animals would come to him to be petted, knowing they were safe. I imagine the radiation of that love must have felt like assurance and shelter to anyone and anything receptive.

Is it possible to feel the safety of home in an age that is marked by terrorism, gun violence, threats of monetary collapse, viral outbreaks and more? I say, Yes.

If the way home was and still is love, it must be universal. Love must be so present, recognizable, and achievable that no matter where we are and no matter what race, religion, or background we profess—whatever our differences—we cannot fail to see it in ourselves and in others.

I've traveled thousands of miles to better know this feeling of home. I now realize that it was always with me. I needed to be still enough and behold it right there inside. Only then would I intimately know it as my very own.

On one of my adventures, I was hitchhiking out of the Four Corners in Arizona headed toward Flagstaff. All of my rides were given by Navajos who travel the long distances over the Colorado Plateau to and from work. I was grateful they were willing to share their beloved earth with me. As evening set in I was dropped off outside a country store way north of Flagstaff.

The San Francisco Peaks loomed miles ahead. I had to get past them to reach Flagstaff. I waited for a while—nothing, not a car passed by. I began to wonder if I would make it. Panic began to set in: No hotel. No room. No shelter. No one to turn to.

The security of my New York City apartment bed came to my mind, but I quickly dismissed it. As I stood on the side of the road gathering myself, the comforting thoughts came, *Wait, you're not lost. You're here. Not where you wanted to be, but you're okay. So why can't this place be home?* I grew calmer. *Yes, this place, as deserted and different as it is, could be home for the night.*

I wandered into the brush and found a place for my sleeping bag under the stars and bedded down. I didn't give snakes or bugs a thought. From that moment on I knew that any place I ever found myself could be, and would be, home.

The feeling of being secure was the groundwork for my hitchhiking around North America, traveling through the Mideast and India, and paving the way for living in Greece.

I moved to Greece to teach meditation. Unbeknownst to me that was only a front. My real purpose was to deepen my sense of home, which I did when I married and became father to my Athenian wife's six-year-old son. When our daughter was born the love nest was complete. Their hearts were the warmth of home like I had never imagined. What they offered not only blessed me but put home at the center of my work.

Our home had a corner room perfectly lit by natural light that I used for my healing practice. As my practice grew, I realized that it wasn't the room itself, our house, or the techniques I used that produced the healings; it was something more subtle and close to heart, the feeling of being safely home. In other words, if a client walked in and felt comforted just being there—as if they were home—then they would let down their guard, be themselves (the real point), and release whatever they had taken on. Voila! Feel at home, find comfort.

One healing illustrated this. A woman came for a session. I had been working with her mother and grandfather with remarkable success. I didn't know what to expect seeing how tightly she was strung. For some reason, I had her sit in a chair in the middle of the room (not a position conducive to relaxing and letting go). She explained to me how while studying in England and under intense mental pressure she had developed a numbness in her wrist that persisted to this day. (Surely, she did not feel home there.) I don't recall the exact words, but I invited her to relax into herself. Then I simply walked her mind out of the tension of the experience in England—unwound her so to speak—showing it was not part of her. The process lasted about fifteen minutes.

That was it. The numbness vanished. We were both in awe.

Whether you are in the familiarity of your house, on a plane 30,000 feet up, or trekking alone in a far-away land, be aware if you are feeling uncomfortable, scared, and simply out of place. If so, stop and gather yourself. Make the space, the people, the sights, and the smells as familiar to you as your own bed. Dwell there completely, give yourself to it, as if no other place on Earth exists and there is no other place you would want to be. Then feel your soul being nourished on all levels.

Let the comfort of your heart welcome you home as it did for me when I was alone in northern Arizona.

THE ARCHKO VOLUME; OR THE ARCHEOLOGICAL WRITINGS OF THE SANHEDRIM AND TALMUDS OF THE JEWS. trans. *Drs. McIntosh and Twyman* (Philadelphia: Antiquarian Book Company, 1905), 94.

DIVINE DEEPENING

Can you be the safe sanctity of home
for the child within, right here, right now?
Tune into that. You will never feel lost again.

Can you void Love
when you hate? No.
Love holds dear
the iciest of hearts.

HER ARMS WERE ALWAYS AROUND ME

When Life doesn't answer my way
What do I do?
Say She isn't listening, and walk away?
Will I get anywhere?
Declare She isn't present, when I refuse
To give my heart?
Find the company of other malcontents
And dwell in 'life sucks'?
Settle for a fickle heart that declares
Life is peace and love one day, and
Conflict and fear the next?

What can I trust in
That never varies
Loves in spite of
Forgives the worst of
Is always available
That never delays
Calls whether I listen or not
Waits with tireless patience, and
Pours forth good perpetually?

One day I'll graciously admit
Her arms were always around me.

DIVINE DEEPENING

God-Spirit-Father-Mother-Life-Source-Love
takes care of your entire existence.
Acknowledge this daily and feel the change.

MEDITATION

Always Home

The quickest way home is to start there. It is not about finally arriving. It is about knowing and claiming you are indeed home. The famous line "There's no place like home" from the screen classic *The Wizard of Oz* rings true in our hearts yet is uttered by a girl who hopes to find herself there. Let's change the hope to certainty in this meditation with "There's no place but home." We never leave because we realize we are always home.

Are you feeling home right this second? Home to yourself? Whether it's yes or no, let's find it together.

Close your eyes. Take a breath into your heart and feel it relax. Let your mind open to the safety of home inside you. What comforting images does that bring up to you that you can always go to? Say to yourself, *I am receiving my divine heritage now. It is with me; it always has been and always will be.* Let yourself be flooded by a secure sense of well-being from those words. Feel grateful that you are dwelling in your eternal home within simply by acknowledging it.

It's that easy. You didn't need to go anywhere, be with anyone, or achieve a certain state. You already possess home, heaven, right in your heart.

Feel the warmth and security of home in your entire being. Begin first in your physical body from your head to your toes. Then feel it fill and balance your emotional/psychic body. Next, see it enlighten your mental/causal body. Finally, let it be embodied in your physical/emotional/mental/spiritual bodies as one, as you. Then let your sense of home go out and out and endlessly out into the universe. You are being home to the universe. The universe is finding home in you. Now say, *My heart is home to the universe*. Really feel that anyone and anything in your existence is home in the center of your heart.

Eventually bring your consciousness back to where you sit or lie. You are home. You are safe. You are at the center of a warm universe. Share that security with the first person you see so they feel home too.

DANCE TO THE DIVINE

IT BOILS DOWN TO CARING

I was playing with the idea of dancing to the Divine the other day and thought, if all of life really is, on some level, a manifestation of the Divine, then I do not want to miss a thing. I want to stay in the dance and see what it holds for me. I don't want to edit my life away from me because it doesn't fit into my preconceived plans of how it must go.

How often do I end up reacting to (even rejecting) the way someone close speaks to me. I don't like their attitude, I get jammed up, and I make a stupid choice. End of receiving. End of communication. No dance to come (see "Self-Justified and Nowhere to Go"). What if a deep, underlying pattern just got triggered in them and the way they spoke was the best they could do? What about me? Did the ego still cloaking (choking) me get triggered? It might have been a golden opportunity to look at myself. Furthermore, it may have set the stage for me to know a deeper aspect of them next time.

I am sure you could think of plenty of events, personal and impersonal, big and small, which you attract daily that present themselves for your undivided attention. Maybe only three in 99 hold some serious growth and discovery for you. But what if the other 96 seeming lightweight invitations to dance eventually lead to greater opportunities in life? All you had to do is say, yes, I am willing to openly tackle anything that comes my way. One of my early spiritual influences Rudi, a.k.a. Albert Rudolph (Swami Rudrananda) of New York created a simple spiritual practice that enabled practitioners to better absorb the essence of whatever experience came their way. This invaluable technique taught me how use the strength of the hara (belly) to keep my heart open and my mind quiet no matter what was in front of me.

One way of looking at any situation is to accept that each experience presents itself for a reason. It is in my face. I don't know what it means yet. But it's here for me to deal with and open to. If I can master myself doing this, what else is possible?

If I had chosen to be upset with my wife because she left so many glass blocks on the window ledge, angry at the cat who was trying to leap up to get at the fish, or ticked off at myself because I stacked the glass blocks right under window frame of glass blocks, then I would have missed a treasure trove of lessons in being gentle. But Grace got ahold of me on the balcony landing as I stood still beholding the glass mess and I knew what I had to do, intimately dance with the glass.

You may still be thinking, how did he know he had to do it the slow, laborious way on all fours? The best I can say is, I yielded, I listened, and I understood. There is one more factor, which in truth supersedes all else. Without it, don't bother. With it, excuses get wiped off the table, resistance fades, and you give your best.

Caring.

In "Soul Offerings," the statement across from one of the poems says, "Either I care, and do or I don't care, and don't do." That ethos covers the whole playing field from morning till night for me. You offer your soul because you care. You are all in, no matter how much work it creates—and it will create plenty—because you are in deeper and will realize what it takes to do a better job and bring quality to everything you do. Especially was this essential for minutely probing between those carpet fibers to extract that last little piece of glass.

A simple story comes to mind that exemplifies this lifestyle that happened years back in the middle of Times Square. I was crossing the intersection of Broadway and 7th Avenue during midday. Being in a hurry, I wouldn't normally look down, but there in the middle of the street was a wallet. I picked it up almost in stride and excitedly opened it on the sidewalk. It was stripped empty, except for a piece of paper. The paper was a deposit slip from a New York bank. I read it and headed for the nearest bank with that name. Once there I showed them the wallet and told them I had found it and only wished to return it and could they could identify who had made the deposit. They did and gave me the name and even the address of where the wallet owner worked. (In today's security-driven world that would probably be a major No No.) I gratefully set off for a midtown office building right off Times Square. The elevator stopped at a very classy office of an international travel magazine. They called the wallet owner out. When I presented her with the wallet she was elated and blown away that someone in the City would do that. I responded, "Even in New York," and left. I wanted to let her know that in such a big, impersonal, fast-moving city there are those who care.

I had had a choice: It's empty, just chuck it (the wallet), or, wouldn't it be cool if I could get it back to the owner. The first was the easy way—keep going, expend no effort, make no connection. The second was the way of caring, and everything that entails. Caring brought out the best in me. Caring connected my heart to life and my heart to hers. Caring is the whole art of life.

When you care, you do. My wife and I share the view that anyone invited into our home is a king or a queen. We prepare our house to be at its absolute best.

It is swept. It is neat. It is aired out. The sumptuous meal fills the air with aroma and is on its way. My children have often been conscripted into our agenda to play their part. I thank them and apologize to them for having weathered our cleaning mania. For the most part, it has been because we care. When you care, you do. You put out your best linens and the most elegant spread. You make every corner of your space open and hospitable. And you open your heart to receive whomever, because you care that they feel welcomed.

That is the art of it. You bring your best consciousness to play where others might have had a lapse. The mindlessly discarded bottle at curbside provides you with the opportunity to prove that care has been entrusted to the right person. You pick up the bottle and dance to the Divine.

FURTHER THOUGHTS

The portraits of a life are living, changing realities. They never end. They segue into higher refinements of character. I liken them to pointers on the way. They make a point and are pointers themselves to something more wondrous and expanded to come. There will always be more portraits, more rites of passage, more subtle insights exploding old myths I hold about myself. I will constantly be waking up from one life and embracing another. I trust that the next and the next will leave me in greater and greater fields of possibilities of what a conscious life has in store for me. That is why I am so excited for anyone who has gone on this journey with me.

Can you dare yourself to imagine the abundance of gems of your life waiting to be picked up, examined, given a shine, and shared with the world. The dance you are in right now may be the very one specially designed for someone out there years down the road. You don't want to miss out on a bit of yourself, so valuable are the experiences you are gathering into your life hopper.

You are loved. You are blessed. You are worth more than all the wealth there is. You are beholding the dearest treasure in the world, You.

Made in the USA
Columbia, SC
13 December 2017